CW01081902

From Where I Sit

ALISON DAVIS

TRIANGLE

First published 1989
Triangle
SPCK
Holy Trinity Church
Marylebone Road
London NW1 4DU

 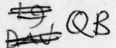
British Library Cataloguing in Publication Data
Davis, Alison
    From where I sit.
    1. Great Britain. Handicapped persons.
    Discrimination by society
    I. Title
    362.4

    I S B N 0–281–04415–5

Photoset by Inforum Typesetting, Portsmouth
Printed in Great Britain by
Hazell Watson & Viney Limited
Member of BPCC plc
Aylesbury Bucks

Contents

Introduction

This book will challenge the way you think about disability. It may well also surprise, shock or embarrass you; but I hope at least that it will prove impossible to ignore what I have to say.

People with physical or mental disabilities have been around for as long as there have been human beings, but most of the time their treatment by the rest of society has been less than good.

Archaeologists have recently discovered early Stone Age skulls on which a kind of crude surgery had been performed. Holes had been drilled into them, intended apparently to release the 'demons' which caused the individuals to act abnormally. To these Stone Age tribes the handicapped were considered a liability. However, nomadic tribes have not necessarily held this view in more recent times. For example, it has been recorded that the Dalegura tribe of Australian aborigines took turns carrying a woman disabled from birth on their backs until she died naturally at the age of sixty-six. They did this because their tradition is never to desert the sick.[1]

Despite the fact that Hippocrates banned killing patients in his ethical statement *The Oath*, the ancient Greeks and Romans generally believed that deformed infants should be quietly got rid of. They did this by exposing them on hillsides if their disability was obvious at birth. If it was not noticed until later the parents were allowed to drown them in the River Tiber. The Jews in these societies were considered most odd because they thought it was a crime to kill *any* child, and it was from their tradition that the Christian doctrine of the sanctity of life was drawn.

St Paul's instruction to comfort the feeble-minded (1 Thessalonians 5.14) was very timely because usually in those days mental handicap, especially epilepsy, was still regarded as satanic possession. In fact, throughout history, there always seems to have been a deep seated fear of those born disabled, and they have usually been thought of as inferior or threatening – objects of society's accumulated fear, hostility and superstition. This is reflected in literature. Can you think of even one book written before this century (or even in this century, come to that) in which someone with an obvious handicap is not considered either a 'deformed monster' or, more recently, as a 'pathetic, helpless cripple'?

For a very short time in the fifteenth century, mentally handicapped people who wandered the streets of many European towns and villages, were called 'Enfants du bon Dieu'. But it was not long before once again these 'children of God' were seen as 'accursed of God' and deserving of no protection, because even God had turned his back on them.

The eighteenth century saw people paying to be entertained by the mentally disordered inmates of Bedlam Hospital, while a hundred years later Charles Darwin wrote in *The Origin of Species*, in which the theory of evolution was developed, that 'feeble mindedness is the mother of crime, pauperism and degeneracy.'

Considering that before the present century the infant mortality rate was phenomenally high, it is not too surprising that few physically handicapped children survived, until hygiene generally began to improve, along with medical knowledge. Thus it was only at the end of the nineteenth century that handicap began to be specifically noticed. Then asylums were widely built for 'lunatics', and the physically handicapped, unless their parents were wealthy, became subject to the Poor Law. This meant they were sent to the infamous workhouses; and if Oliver Twist had a bad time there, it is not hard to imagine what the fate of handicapped inmates must have been.

The trouble lay mainly with the fact that giving birth to a handicapped child was still generally regarded as a punishment from God, so not unnaturally parents were usually very keen to keep such children hidden away at home, out of sight and, to some extent at least, out of mind. Even when special schools for handicapped children began to be set up, many parents were at first reluctant to allow their children, particularly girls, to attend.

Nowadays society seems to congratulate itself on magnanimously viewing the disabled as ill rather than as victims of divine retribution. However, as I hope this book will demonstrate, it is really a bit soon to be complacent.

If you think the end of the Second World War saw the last killing of those deemed 'socially undesirable', think again. More than forty years later, unborn handicapped babies are regularly detected and aborted, and sometimes the newborn are sedated and starved to death. Some people think this is merciful, others that it is simply economic. You might be forgiven for thinking the following came out of the Nazi propaganda machine:

> The grossly handicapped spina bifida child and adult make large demands on the health and social services. The cost of these demands exceed the cost of a programme to detect the condition [in time for abortion].

Actually, it comes from a DHSS pamphlet entitled *Prevention and Health: Everyone's Business*. The only real difference between killing the handicapped in medieval times, and doing it in the twentieth century is that then it was performed by the lowest and least reputable members of society. Now it is done by those generally considered to be among the 'pillars of the community' – doctors.

Despite apparent advances in the treatment of disabled people by society, especially since the 1981 International Year of Disabled People, there are still enormous barriers to our integration: inaccessible homes and buildings, and transport systems, prejudice in education, in employment, and restricted access to places of entertainment. In many ways the struggle for equality by disabled people can be seen as the last civil rights battle.

So why should Christians be particularly concerned about this? There are several very good reasons. Christians believe that human life is a gift, and that we should not presume to judge that some lives were mistakes on the part of God. The Bible also teaches that we should love our neighbour, and it does not add the convenient proviso 'so long as he isn't disabled, sick or ill'.

As we have seen, throughout history disabled people have been picked on, feared and reviled; nowadays this fear may be less obvious, but the increasing enthusiasm for detecting and aborting disabled people as early as possible proves that such attitudes have yet to be adequately put to rest.

I hope this book will help persuade you that there is actually no need to fear disability. It is just another fact of human life, and one which ought not to be ignored. There are some things which disabled people can teach the able bodied, and vice versa. We should be considered equal partners in this learning, not as respectively superior and inferior beings.

Sudden handicap can strike anyone, something most able bodies people dread. But even if this kind of tragedy does not happen, almost everyone will eventually get older and less able. It is important to recognise this, and learn to face it without fear. The Hindu Janet says that 'The poor and sick should be regarded as Lords of the atmosphere.' It is about time Christians remembered that Jesus himself taught that the disabled have a particular, and special purpose in life (John 9.3).

Both individual Christians and churches need to respond to this challenge. No person should be excluded from a church, either by lack of welcome, or by lack of access. New church buildings must always have access for disabled people; it is sobering to think what the inaccessibility of old churches says about attitudes to the status of the handi-capped in past times.

We who are handicapped want, and need, to be able to participate in all the church's activities, not be relegated always to 'special' services and facilities, which only serve to segregate us more.

The greatest need of all, however, is that you take time to listen and reflect on the needs, desires and aspirations of people with disabilities.

It is always important to be able to offer time to listen to other people and hear what is to be told. We cannot ever cross the divide between ourselves and others; but we can pay attention to what they tell us they see on their side.[2]

1

People with Disabilities

What does it mean to be a person with a disability? It is a question which will run right through this book. As a start it is probably a good idea to look at the kind of experiences which can affect the personalities of disabled people, their relationships, and their assimilation into society.

The words 'disability' or 'handicap' are really just general terms, used to describe a large number of people who have in common only one thing – that they don't function in quite the same way as those considered to be 'normal'. In most ways we are just the same as the able bodied, but both our disabilities and society's attitude to them can have a tremendous effect on our self-confidence and sense of worth.

The earliest development of human beings begins before they are even born; a fact which is known to almost everyone now. Expectant mothers often comment that their unborn children react differently to different sorts of music – perhaps being pacified by Beethoven, and aroused to frantic kicking by Status Quo! There is also some learning before birth. Newborn babies respond best to the sound of their mother's voice, the one they have heard most often in the womb. As a result of this the babies of deaf parents invariably have an unusual, distinctive cry, because of the way their mothers speak.

Newborn babies spend their first few months learning to distinguish themselves from other people, and recognising others as separate, permanent beings. Later they learn to recognise themselves in mirrors, and gradually to relate to other people and eventually to play with them. Then they begin to understand the world outside the immediate home, and the fact that they can influence it in some ways. They hear stories, and watch other children at play, or on television, which excites different possibilities in them.

All these experiences are slightly different for children with disabilities, though not always in obvious ways. Blind children often take longer to learn their identity, because they cannot see themselves in mirrors. Parents need to first establish effective communication with deaf children before the process of learning about the world can really begin. And those with mentally handicapped children need to be shown how best to maximise their offspring's potential and abilities.

On a less immediate level, it is interesting to consider what normal children learn from stories, pictures and children's TV programmes. They learn that there are other children like them, who do different things; that they can participate in exciting adventures; and that they will one day grow up and be like the adults they see around them. A physically handicapped child learns rather different things from those same stories.

There are very few modern books which realistically portray the lives of handicapped children, so they learn very early on that they are unusual, and that the children they see and read about having adventures do not have disabilities. None of the adults in books or on children's programmes apparently have disabilities either; so, particularly if the child is the only disabled one in the family, he may well begin to wonder if in fact he is the only such person in the world. Handicapped children need role models, if anything even more than the able bodied. This was actually provided rather well in the 1960s by the wheelchair detective, Ironside. He was definitely a hero to be emulated, and it was probably only those like me with a cynical nature who wondered why all the criminals he caught lived conveniently on the ground floor!

It is probably partly as a result of this scarcity of examples in the media that some handicapped children come to regard the able bodied as 'perfect' and themselves as inferior. Too big a difference between an ideal body image and our own body image is psychologically unhealthy, and needs to be counteracted. There are, after all, many examples of handicapped people who have grown up to lead ordinary, or even exciting, lives – the great need is for handicapped children, their parents and society in general to realise this.

Studies show that as many as 50 per cent of the population have primarily negative attitudes to disability, something I hope this book will help to remedy. Those who are to some extent prejudiced tend to shun not just the disabled, but also any member of a group which can be classed as 'different' – black people, those of a different class or religion, mentally ill people, ex-prisoners, etc. And it seems that their attitude tends to worsen the closer such people get to them; for instance if a handicapped, or black, person is asking them for a job, or wants to marry into their family.

The use of outdated terms to describe disabilities – moron, mongol, spastic, cripple – tends to make such prejudices even more apparent. As Merry Cross who has a deformed, very short leg, says: 'So much language about disability is negative – like "What's *wrong* with you?" "Why is your leg *bad*?" People talk of us as invalids; in-valid.'[1]

Everyone has heard of severely disabled people being described as 'human vegetables'; but no one calls tall thin people 'human carrots' or those who are short and fat 'potato beings'. Why are disabled people the only ones to be referred to in horticultural terms? It can only be because to some extent the people who say such things think we *are* actually somewhat less than fully human.

The lack of positive disabled role models can often lead to unnecessary anguish. Handicapped adolescents, seeing others dating or going out to discos, tend to assume they will never be able to do the same, simply because they have never heard of anyone like them who does. Obviously coming to terms with reality is important, and facing up to being disabled is a vital part of growing up; but so is the knowledge that disabled adults do ordinary and extraordinary things, just like the able bodied.

I suppose I first realised my handicap in the last year of my Infants' School. My mother came in every day to change my nappies, and I can remember getting very upset about it, because no one else's mother came to school. It was not long after that that I learned to change them myself, so the problem was to some extent overcome (although I was always apprehensive, until I had my urinary diversion operation at the age of thirteen, that other pupils would discover my 'difference'.) For those physically incapable of such feats, however, the problem would remain, and would require a lot of sensitive positive counselling to overcome.

Pupils at special schools usually do not realise that they are handicapped until a later stage, since they are not really 'different' from others in their class; but eventually awareness has to come to every disabled person.

Although I am a strong believer in the value of integrated education, I do think it is important for handicapped children to meet others with disabilities, both children and adults, in order to realise that their problems are not unique and that they will not always be the 'odd one out'. For me this was very happily achieved by being taken by my parents to a swimming club for handicapped people, where I met others with disabilities, some a lot more severe than mine. I also met mentally handicapped people there, which was fortuitous. So many physically handicapped people, especially those who become disabled later in life, feel a need to assert their relative 'normality' by constantly separating themselves from the mentally handicapped. My early experiences at the swimming club enabled me to view all handicapped people as just ordinary people with enormous individual potential and worth. This realisation is an education in itself.

Another result of always being in a sense 'marginalised' is that some handicapped children have completely unrealistic aspirations for the future. As an example I admit, somewhat bashfully, that throughout my childhood I was convinced I would end up as a ballet dancer. My mother very sensibly told me that I shouldn't be surprised if this did not turn out to be true, as not many people manage it anyway – a very sound tactic.

Parents are sometimes subject to this kind of thing, but in reverse, when they are first told their child is handicapped. Several parents of congenitally handicapped boys have told me that the paediatrician said to them 'Your son will never play football for England.' It takes time and the ability to stand back from the situation for a moment, to realise that the answer to this is 'So what?' To quote William Bee, who has spina bifida:

> Maybe your disabled son can't play ordinary football, but wheelchair football is a considerably more skillful game anyway. Maybe we can't run a four minute mile, but how many able bodied people could do 450 yards in a wheelchair in four minutes fifteen seconds, as I can?[2]

(If this does not sound too impressive, may I suggest you borrow a wheelchair and try it!)

I am not minimising the problems of parents who have to decide, say, how much to stress the importance of walking even if it is very tiring; or how much to concentrate on developing the handicapped child's development at the possible expense of attention for his fit brothers and sisters; or whether to allow signing for a deaf child, or to insist on speech. But this is a book about people who have disabilities, and our main concerns are about how best we and other people can be accepting of our unchangeable conditions, while at the same time acknowledging the need for us to fit easily into our families and communities.

An important element in the development of a healthy self-concept is to define our own role in the world. Since disabilities rarely permeate every aspect of an individual's life, other factors will be equally important in deciding how a person views his own role. Handicapped people are born randomly into loving or broken homes, and will enjoy the advantages, or suffer the consequences, of each in the same way as any other children. Likewise, some families will consider even a minor disability a disaster, while others find quite major handicaps no problem at all. One genetic counsellor when answering a questionnaire claimed that for herself she would accept 'nothing short of perfection' in her children. On the other hand, Jane and Eifon Saunders say:

> Our two year old son Ben who has Down's Syndrome does not suffer in any way. I remember one person saying that we would get upset when we went to the clinic and

saw the other normal babies. Not so. We felt sorry for the other parents whose babies were not as handsome as ours.[3]

Nevertheless there are undoubtedly problems, especially for physically handicapped children, in developing a healthy positive self image. Those who have unco-ordinated movements often miss out on some forms of learning – picking things up, exploring around the house, etc – and if they also lack the capacity to speak they will initially be reduced to crying or yelling for attention – behaviour normally associated with babies – even if they have normal intelligence.

Blind children generally have difficulty at first in learning concepts which are abstract or intangible (behind, between, among, the sky, clouds), and deaf children very frequently have behavioural problems simply because of their inability to communicate effectively. This can also apply to some mentally handicapped children.

Incontinence is always a major source of problems for those affected by it. Boys having their penile appliances changed by their mothers or female hospital or school staff, and girls being changed by their fathers, can suffer much stress, largely because it seems like a throwback to infantile dependency. The same is also true for those people who need help with feeding and dressing. An additional anxiety is shown by some handicapped adolescents and adults who feel unable to argue or come into conflict with those they depend on for physical care.

Try to imagine for a moment what it would be like to depend for your every physical need on someone towards whom you feel angry or bitter. Every adolescent sometimes feels this way about their parents and those in authority; but the handicapped need to think a good deal more carefully than the able bodied before voicing what they are actually feeling. How would *you* cope in this situation? Would you grin and bear it (which might well do you some psychological damage, or at the very least cause your tongue to suffer a lot of biting)? Would you lash out and subsequently regret it (maybe very deeply, and with long lasting consequences)?

Finding an acceptable alternative to these two extremes is essential, but very difficult.

The basic emotional needs of every human being are security, affection, acceptance, self expression and from time to time a sense of achievement. Everyone needs to be allowed to take some risks in life (even if, as in my case, this sometimes entails putting up with broken bones). Equally well, we all need to be subject to some rules and discipline, and parents who let children 'get away with' things because they are disabled do them no favours at all.

In the development of normal children, games with fixed rules are very important, and they quickly appreciate the concepts of 'fair' and 'unfair'. Even if a handicapped child cannot totally understand what the games mean (one of my favourite characters, Daniel Brown, who has Down's Syndrome, has the habit of signing 'We've *all* won' at the end of games), it is important that they are not spoilt or allowed to become self centred or boastful. To quote William Bee again:

> From my experience at a school for the handicapped I know that if children spend as little as a week with relatives who spoil them, they need to be taught even how to tie their shoelaces again.[4]

The problem is, though, that rules are sometimes not quite so clear cut for handicapped people, and uncertainties abound. For instance, 'Don't tell lies' is a sound general rule; but does that mean you have to tell the complete truth to every nosey parker about being incontinent? Yet if it is acceptable to relax the general rule in special instances like that, how can handicapped children be sure which rules *do* apply to them, and which don't? Most children can work out their frustrations and uncertainties by acting them out with dolls or toys, but these particular worries are often too complex for that. They don't stop at childhood either.

Disabled people are sometimes allowed free into places of interest or museums, and most able bodied people seem to think it must be wonderful to have such a privilege. But is it really? It usually only means an exacerbation of uncertain-

7

ties – whenever you go out you have to wonder, 'Will I be allowed in: a) at all? b) free (and if so, does this mean I can only visit certain parts of the building)? c) paying the normal fee? Yet we fear to phone ahead and enquire to resolve this dilemma, in case it somehow suggests we think we *ought* to be let in free. We never seem to be able to assume that we will be regarded by others as having ordinary personalities, and relationships with other people.

A very sad example of this kind of uncertainty in role was told to me by a handicapped teenager:

> When my able bodied sister, who is younger than me, tells our Granny to sit down and have a rest, she does so smiling. But if I say the same thing, she gets angry, and says, '*You* shouldn't tell me what to do.'

Fear of failure is a big problem for many handicapped people, maybe because their limitations are often viewed in this light. They may become so anxious to avoid failing that they never attempt new tasks, and thus can seem completely indecisive (though sometimes this may also have a simple explanation – some handicapped people would find it hard to decide when it is safe to cross a road, simply because they have never been allowed to do it alone). Mentally handicapped people, for instance, sometimes need to relearn skills in each new environment, and so the fact that they can successfully have a bath at home does not necessarily mean they could also do so in a different place, like a hotel, where the layout is completely altered.

Since working on Independence courses for handicapped teenagers, I have learned that 'backward chaining' is often a good way to get around this. It works like this, for making a cup of tea: *Day 1*, pour out tea someone else has made. *Day 2*, put milk and sugar in cup, then pour out tea. *Day 3*, fill teapot from kettle, put milk and sugar in cup, pour out tea. *Day 4*, put kettle on to boil, fill teapot, etc. The crucial thing is that every day ends with the successful drinking of a cup of tea.

If this kind of thing is not taught, the pressure of knowing the awful consequences of failure may make some disabled children crack up or give up, and there are very many examples of this in daily life.

The greatest need of disabled people, however, is simply to be regarded as what we are – ordinary human beings with the same social and emotional needs as others. So often handicapped people are assumed not to want to do ordinary things, like going to parties, visiting pubs, getting married, driving a car, having children – and after years of being left out, some may end up using the excuse, 'I didn't want to anyway', as a kind of defence mechanism. We need to be allowed enough self confidence to say, 'Don't leave me out! I want to do it too!'

The same qualities that make an able bodied person attractive as a friend – sociability, being fun to be with, having good ideas – also hold true for the handicapped; but unless a healthy self image has developed, it is much harder for us to be relaxed enough to be like this.

One of the most traumatic experiences for any handicapped child is the separation from parents caused by being in hospital. I have spent quite a lot of time in hospital over the years, and even now I can remember the awful loneliness and fear I felt being there as a child. I was certainly more fortunate than many, as my parents always visited every day, and told me exactly when they would come back; but the knowledge that, however hard you cry, they will not come back NOW is very hard. This is especially true when the child begins to appreciate that unpleasant things happen in hospital, usually when the parents have gone away.

Some parents, of course, just cannot visit every day, if they have other commitments, or other children to look after. Nowadays, however, at least most parents are given the chance to stay with their child if it is possible for them to do so, and this is bound to result in much less strain. It also helps to counteract the uncertainty and worry caused by a change of routine, and being looked after by different nurses when shifts change. The National Association for the Welfare of Children in Hospital has made these great advances possible, and as a result handicapped children will probably be much better able to cope with their enforced periods in hospital than those of my generation were.

Even so, when first coming out of hospital, especially if the stay has been long, many children can be difficult – irritable and angry, or clinging and anxious, and reluctant to let mother out of their sight for even a minute. These are usually temporary wounds, however, and the love of family and friends can help heal them. Dr Jennifer Gray, mother of Susan who has spina bifida and hydrocephalus, says:

> Whatever her handicap and its problems, at least she knows the most important thing of all – God's love, and the love of her family and those who help care for her.[5]

Both handicapped children and their parents can sometimes achieve amazing things, given this kind of dedication and love. Linda Scotson was told that her brain damaged son Doran, who was deaf, blind, dumb and had unco-ordinated movements would be a 'cabbage'. She refused to accept this, and now he talks, walks, reads aloud and writes. He is attending an ordinary school. Yet without the love and determination of his mother, his potential might have remained forever dormant.[6]

Such transformations are not always possible, of course; but what is quite attainable is a sensible, positive attitude towards disability. To encourage this I always try to persuade visitors to my house to have a go in my wheelchair, and discover for themselves that it alters only their mobility, not their humanity. Yes, disabled people do have problems, and sometimes need physical and emotional support, but at heart we are not that different. Edna Pesall, who has Huntington's Chorea puts it in a nutshell: 'The things I cannot do are not failures; they are just some of the things I can live without.'[7]

The biggest worry for many handicapped teenagers is what will happen when they grow up – will they be able to lead ordinary emotional and sexual lives? It can be very difficult to discuss this with their parents, who in any case probably don't know either.

Unfortunately the quality of sex education most teenagers are given in schools is poor, particularly at special schools. Often it is either inappropriate to their special concerns, or completely non-existent. Sadly, also, some able bodied people have strange ideas, and consider that people with disabilities should not marry at all, or should only marry another disabled person – or they even assume that we are totally asexual.

I was married for ten years to an able bodied man, before being divorced three years ago. I can recall quite clearly the common reaction of strangers that we must be brother and sister; that surely I could not be his wife! My husband was often seen as something of a martyr for marrying me (and then as unspeakably inhuman and cruel when he left me), but I cannot share this attitude. It was an ordinary relationship, which went wrong. The break-up was a trauma which affected me profoundly; in fact it still does, but I think that is generally true of most divorces, whether or not one partner or both are disabled.

Unfortunately, the Christian churches are not always as understanding as they should be about relationships for the disabled. A Catholic priest refused initially to marry one couple because the man, an ex-soldier, was considered to be impotent, and therefore incapable of fathering children. He had to go through the humiliation of a medical examination before the marriage was finally allowed to go ahead. It can easily be imagined what this did to his psychological well-being.

When the couple first met, this man said that he did believe in God – 'Who doesn't turn to him in their time of need?' – though he added, 'But how can you praise the Lord for a broken neck?' His treatment by the Church was hardly conducive to a successful resolution of this question.[8]

There often seems to be a great curiosity amongst the able bodied about how disabled people function in normal relationships, if indeed they can be said to function at all. I have frequently been asked by complete strangers (particularly on trains, for some reason!) 'Can you have children?' And I remember very well a doctor at the university health centre when I was a student, answering my request for a prescription of the Pill by asking, 'But how do you do it?' My response was to ask her in turn how she did it, which predictably she refused to tell me!

11

Sometimes handicapped people are assumed only to be capable of forming relationships with other disabled people, which leads a few to think that this must inevitably be true. In the book *Women with Disabilities Talking: Images of Ourselves*, Angie writes:

I was about fourteen and had just finished preparing a salad in the cookery class. The teacher came over and said, 'What a good job you have made of that. You would have made someone a good wife.' 'What do you mean, I would have?' I asked. 'Well,' she replied, 'What I meant to say was, if you marry a disabled man, you would make him a good wife.'

The fact is, of course, that many disabled people do have close physical relationships, sometimes with other handicapped people, sometimes with the able bodied. The vital factor, as with any relationship, is tolerance and acceptance by both partners. Sue and Bob Flaherty in the USA both have spina bifida, and have a son, John, now aged three.[9] Louise and John Medus also have a baby. He is partially sighted, and she has no arms or legs – a thalidomide-induced disability. Louise comments: 'We're an odd sight when we go out. I push the pram, and John pushes me!'[10]

Micheline Mason, a single parent, has brittle bones and can walk with crutches, although she often uses a wheelchair. She is three feet tall. Her daughter Lucy Rose has the same condition. Micheline explains: 'I always dreamed I would have a baby, but never, never spoke about it. Whilst growing up everyone assumed that because of my terrible condition, I wouldn't have a boyfriend, much less sex and babies, and to some degree I believed them.' Finally a woman doctor told her, 'You can have a baby if you want to. There is a 50 per cent chance the baby would also be affected, but so what? We treat them better now than in your day.'[11] This absolutely excellent attitude is very rare, but heartening for every disabled person.

Micheline's pregnancy was unplanned, but welcome, and the paediatrician commented after the birth, 'Of course there has never been a baby better prepared for, because

Micheline knows all about the condition.' Micheline says, 'In getting things right for Lucy Rose I see all the ways in which I had accepted less than the best for myself. She is the perfect baby for me because in learning to completely love her, I am learning to completely love myself.'

The problems faced by mentally handicapped people are similar, but more pronounced and more difficult. The issue of sterilising mentally handicapped women has been in the news in recent years, as well as the sad case of Mr and Mrs Morgan, a mentally handicapped couple, whose baby was taken into care immediately after the birth. They were allowed one last visit, but will not be allowed to see him again.[12] Naturally the interests of the child must come first but many people considered they could have coped, with help.

Another case, with a happier ending, was that of Pat Tanner, a mentally handicapped woman now in her sixties, who became pregnant thirty years ago. The baby, Frances, was cared for by her grandparents, and now Pat lives with Frances and her family. Pat, who has a mental age of five, has just been taught to read – by her daughter![13]

Parents quite naturally worry about the welfare of their disabled children, particularly if they have a mental handicap. However, denying them the joys and sorrows of physical relationships is surely not the answer. The organisation Christian Care for the Mentally Handicapped observes that: 'Sexuality is something which mentally handicapped people have in common with us all, as part of their humanity. It cannot and should not be rubbed out. The handicapped need to be taught about appropriate behaviour just like any normal adolescent.'[14] Peter and Ann Realf, who decided that their twenty-four-year-old Down's daughter Bernadette should not be sterilised said:

We feel that it does not solve the many problems parents face in this dilemma. It certainly does not protect them from the serious hazards of sexual abuse and disease. It may even encourage the abuse of a sterilised girl, because the abuser has no 'result' to worry about.[15]

13

Handicap does cause some problems, there is no doubt of that. But there is also no doubt that it has compensations too, and that there *is* a purpose in suffering and disability, even though it is often hard to see and still harder to understand. Mother Julian of Norwich knew about this: 'You would know our Lord's meaning in this? Know it well. Love was His meaning.'

2

The Right to Learn

I suppose most people, if asked to react to the word 'education' would conjure up a mental picture of children being taught in a classroom. The children might represent very different backgrounds, and be of all sizes, shapes and colours, but very rarely would the group include a child with an obvious disability.

So few able bodied people have any direct contact with anyone disabled that for the most part they simply tend to forget about our existence, unless they are specifically asked to think about disability. Yet maybe one in ten people are handicapped in some way. So why have so few able bodied people come into contact with them? And would it have been beneficial if they had?

We are supposed to have 'comprehensive' education now, but of course it cannot really be comprehensive until it includes everyone. Unfortunately, though, that is not too likely to happen until there is generally a more understanding and tolerant attitude to those who are physically or mentally different.

Among my very earliest memories are painful incidents when I was asked by other children (and sometimes also by adults) 'What's wrong with you?' Now, I suppose, I would dispute that my disability is something 'wrong', but at the time this was a terribly difficult question, which I generally tried to ignore as much as I could. In fact, I'm not at all sure I know even now *why* I am disabled – I just have to accept that this is how I was made. I believe it has a purpose, but I don't know yet (indeed I may never really know) what that purpose is. It is only relatively recently that I have started to consider other people's questions about my disability in a dispassionate way, and to wonder about the mentality that provokes them.

Everyone internalises to a certain extent what other people say about them. A child who is very beautiful, or very clever, and has been told so often enough, will generally grow up to believe it, which boosts their self confidence. That in turn tends to make them seem even more beautiful or clever. Likewise, the things a disabled person is told most often eventually stick, and become part of that person's own self image. Sadly, in the case of disability, these things are often negative, which in the end come to be accepted as true.

It is important to think about those negative questions a bit more closely. What, after all, is 'wrong' about being disabled, except that it is sometimes rather a disadvantage to have to rely on other people, or on a wheelchair, or glasses, or hearing aids? What is 'wrong' with being mentally handicapped, other than needing help with some things that other people can do for themselves, which might sometimes cause frustration?

In fact, if we took a more positive attitude, there is a lot that could be considered 'good' about disability. The mentally handicapped, for instance, are very unlikely to harm other people or their property, and the physically handicapped are not likely to grow up to kill or be killed in a war.

The whole history of the segregation of disabled people has been based on fear. Handicap has been often seen as the fault of the parents, who should therefore hide away with their guilt; or handicapped people are viewed as being completely different from everyone else, and only really fit to be 'with their own kind'. It is this sort of attitude which has led many disabled people to feel that the only thing society finds interesting about them is their disability.

I am not infrequently described, particularly by doctors, as 'a spina bifida' as if it was part of my personality, rather than a description of part of my body. I am no more 'a spina bifida' than I am sometimes 'a headache' or 'a cold'. No one would say of a non-handicapped person, 'Meet my friend John. He's a runny nose!' All I ask is that I and those like me be treated with equal respect. We are not a different species after all; we have the same feelings and need of acceptance as other people.

It is high time that able bodied society began to realise this

16

fact and act upon it. Their fear needs to be confronted. It is as needless as a fear of black people, or of foreigners. All of us have our abilities and disabilities, our gifts and our problems. No one should presume to judge who is 'better'; but rather we should all appreciate that no one is born without a purpose.

Young children do not necessarily share these attitudes. If we were to ask pupils at those schools which do integrate handicapped children what place there is for the disabled in our community, I am sure their answer would be very different from that of people who have never experienced the realities of handicap. These children are much more likely to accept handicapped people for what they are, and to be realistic about their differences.

Take, for instance, the views of the nine-year-old classmates of Samantha Hulley, a severely multi-handicapped girl. Sam is mentally handicapped, unable to walk or speak and is also partially sighted. When asked 'Do you think of Sam as someone very different from you,' the children answered:

'No, not really.'

'Well, the first time you think so, but once you get to know her it's O K. You think of her as a normal person.'

'It was hard to get used to it, but once you got used to it, I liked it myself. I think it gave more . . . it would be boring if there wasn't anyone, you know . . . like I think it's more adventurous with people like that.'[1]

I can't see any good reason why more able bodied and handicapped children should not be able to enjoy this mutually beneficial experience. Nevertheless, some do argue against it.

One mother of a spina bifida child has very decided views:

I prefer my son to be one of the top dogs in his school, rather than an underdog in a normal school. Incontinent children will be grossly ridiculed and segregated in an integrated situation, quite apart from the physical

17

dangers of being left out of social groups. There is also the problem of missing schooling due to hospital visits and stays, physiotherapy and general illness.[2]

But do all these problems add up to a need for special segregated schools? If there was proper provision in all schools for the special educational and physical needs of handicapped children, including simple straightforward explanations of the problems to other pupils, and facilities to help the handicapped catch up after absence, couldn't these difficulties and objections be overcome? I think they could.

To artificially segregate able bodied children, denying them access to anyone with a disability, and then expect them to care about and understand disabled people later in life, is quite unfair and totally unrealistic. No wonder many able bodied people feel embarrassed and ill at ease when they meet someone handicapped for the first time. It is all very well to urge that Christians should be aware of the needs of their 'neighbours', be they next door or in another continent; but first we have to know that they exist and that they need some degree of help.

This ignorance and embarrassment about disability manifests itself in different ways, all of which create acute problems for people with handicaps. Complete strangers will come up and ask me 'What's wrong?' as if they had a right to know, and they may get very annoyed if I reply that I think it is rather rude of them to ask. Often what they really want to know is if I will 'get better' (i.e. if I am to be categorised as 'normal' or not), and most find the answer 'No' hard to accept. What I want to tell them is that actually it doesn't much matter to me. Of course I would rather not be disabled, but there are things I want more in life than to be physically 'better' – such as to travel more, to be a better, more caring, more compassionate person, to understand the world and the things in it more fully. Able bodied people find this difficult to believe, maybe because they are still seeing me as 'a spina bifida' who must want to be something other than that. But of course I am already something other than that! I am Alison Davis, who has much to contribute to the world, but still has a lot to learn.

18

The apparently overwhelming need of some people to know the whys and wherefores of disability is, I suspect, largely due to simple lack of experience. No one bothers, after all, to ask people who wear glasses 'What's wrong?'; or gets upset to discover that the person will always have to wear them. The obvious answer to 'Why do you wear glasses?' is 'Because my eyes are weak and they help me see clearly.' Similarly the answer to 'Why are you in a wheel-chair?' is obviously 'Because my legs are weak, and it helps me get about.' No one thinks of asking the person with glasses 'Why?' because there are so many people who wear them, everyone is used to it; and the problem is not regarded as a major misfortune. When one thinks of the proportion of disabled people in society – ten per cent – this ought to be true of all disabling conditions.

If I lived in a society where being in a wheelchair was no more remarkable than wearing glasses, and if the community was completely accepting and accessible, my disability would be an inconvenience and not much more than that. It is society which handicaps me, far more seriously and completely than the fact that I have spina bifida. The same is sadly not true of disabled people in many Third World countries, simply because the means of overcoming their limitations are too expensive to afford. In many poor countries short sight can mean a lifetime of begging or being supported by the family, because glasses are beyond the reach of most ordinary people. In view of this, I think it would be fair to say that I am fortunate for having a wheelchair to use, rather than unfortunate for needing one.

It is particularly important for Christians to appreciate the truth of what I am trying to say. I cannot believe that my disability was just a mistake, a product of one of God's off days. Jesus himself, when he healed the man who was born blind (John 9.3), stressed that handicap is not the fault of the individual or the family, but rather exists so that God's glory may be made manifest. To try to pretend otherwise is to deny one of the most profound truths of creation.

Unfortunately, though, life can seem one long obstacle course to disabled people and their families, with the ob-stacles largely set up by an unknowing and uncaring society.

And this is nowhere more obvious than in the education system, where parents often have to fight against very heavy odds to have their handicapped children educated in ordinary schools. Ann Bailey, whose son Ben has Down's Syndrome was told he must go to a special school for the mentally handicapped, but Ann felt he had got on so well in an ordinary playgroup that he would be held back in a segregated environment. So Ann fought against the decision of the Education Department, and won.[3] Many Down's children are now being educated in ordinary schools, and proving that it was well worth giving them the chance to try.

However, because of the enormous problems some parents encounter, many feel that if only their child were less handicapped, integration might be more possible. This has contributed to the great enthusiasm for Conductive Education, and hundreds of handicapped children have now been taken to Hungary to benefit from the system there. In fact it has proved so popular that it is likely a similar scheme will eventually be provided in Britain. The idea is to encourage handicapped children to achieve the maximum degree of independence possible; and some amazing achievements have indeed been attained. I do think, however, that a sense of proportion must be kept, and parents and therapists should remember that handicapped children are still children. They need to have fun and games as well as hard work, and to concentrate sometimes on things other than their disabilities.

That even very severely handicapped children can fit into ordinary schools, given a flexible tolerant attitude by staff and pupils, was shown very clearly by the experiences of Christopher Nolan, author of the award winning autobiography *Under The Eye of The Clock*. Christopher attended an ordinary school despite having cerebral palsy and being unable to speak. His book describes his life at school, and no one reading it can be left in any doubt that both he and the rest of the pupils benefited greatly from each other.

I was fortunate always to attend ordinary schools, despite my disability and the numerous hospital visits and stays it entailed. On the whole I am sure it was best, in that I learned to cope with being different in an environment designed for the able bodied, at the same time as getting what is generally called a 'good education'. That is not to say, though, that there were no problems.

Being disabled and doubly incontinent in an unknowing and largely uncaring atmosphere creates sometimes intolerable pressure. How could I explain leaking nappies or urine bags to people who didn't even know I wore them? Or the difficulties of catching up after long absences in hospital, where at times my dignity and sense of self esteem had been seriously damaged? Or the degree of sheer physical tiredness which I often felt because the geography of the building necessitated an immense output of energy, and reliance on sometimes unwilling classmates? Very often, of course, people were helpful, and most of the time I fitted in well; but uncertainties were always there at the back of my mind – uncertainties which still occasionally preoccupy me now.

I never knew whether or not the staff were aware of my problems, but the other pupils certainly only knew what was obvious. I worried almost all the time about the possibility of them finding out about my incontinence – I suppose I felt it was somehow shameful, yet I never felt the same way about the weakness of other muscles. Maybe this is just a reflection of society's attitude that incontinence is much less 'acceptable' than mobility problems. I wonder if the other girls would have been understanding, or, as I feared, would have ridiculed me mercilessly and made my life unbearable. I suppose I will never know now.

I did learn two very valuable lessons from my school experience. The first was how to cope with extraordinarily difficult physical and emotional problems, so that they would remain hidden from the prying eyes of an already discriminatory society. And secondly, that the things we find intolerable about ourselves are hardly amenable to rational discussion with others; which is why I have made a conscious effort to overrule the reluctance I feel even now about mentioning incontinence.

To put it another way, which is perhaps clearer, I must first accept that this is me, as God made me and intended me to be, before I can claim to be a whole equal person, and educate other people to regard me as such. This is difficult because handicapped people are all the time fighting against the prejudice of those who consider themselves 'normal' and us 'abnormal'. But they are not necessarily right just because they are in the majority.

This is the message which all children, handicapped or not, ought to be receiving from their teachers and from society as a whole – that they are acceptable just as they are. No one person is intrinsically worse or better than others at being or becoming what they already are – human beings. We all have our difficulties, and these need to be recognised and worked on; but what is important in the final analysis is that we should all see ourselves and others as individuals with potentials and capabilities which are unique to the person concerned. What we all share are the same basic rights and responsibilities of humanity.

After taking my 'O' and 'A' levels at school, I went on to Essex University, where I read sociology. There, for the first time, I felt fully accepted as an equal, and it was a new and exhilarating experience to be able at last to concentrate on things other than my physical limitations. Unlike school, the university buildings were all wheelchair accessible, and no one was patronising or discriminatory. I was enabled to see disability from the perspective of a political issue of minority rights, and to understand that discrimination on the grounds of handicap stems from the same fears and prejudices as racism or sexism. For the first time I could accept who and what I was without having constantly to struggle to be seen as what I obviously was not – able bodied.

Since then I have realised how very important the struggle for equal rights is. Until society as a whole comes to realise that, just like everyone else, we ought to be free to participate in and contribute to humanity, we will go on being downtrodden, ignored or treated as inferior.

Education is not simply something one 'gets' or undergoes at school. It is a lifelong process of growth and development; but it needs to have a sound beginning if it is to be healthy and productive. So what is the Christian approach to the education, in the fullest sense of the word, of handicapped people? In the past, disabled children have been seen as objects of 'charity', for whom education was a privilege rather than as a right. 'Charity' has become a devalued word, to such an extent that accepting it is often regarded as a failure on the part of the individual on the receiving end. It is not only old people who think that 'accepting charity' is the ultimate degradation, to be avoided at all costs. Yet if we remember the words of St Paul, we see that treating our fellow human beings with charity is a duty and not an option.

Paul's famous passage on charity (love) in 1 Corinthians 13 puts the responsibility firmly on us. It is for us to treat others in a charitable way, rather than for them simply to 'accept charity' in a passive sense, without having at the same time the opportunity themselves to contribute to a charitable environment. Charity means love of our fellow human beings, kindness, affection, beneficence and giving ourselves to those in need and distress. There is a duty on everyone, including the handicapped, not just to receive it gracefully, but also to give it, in whatever way we can. We have no right to segregate those who, we think, need to receive more of it than they can give. Because what they do have to give can be profound, spectacular, and essential to the development of a just, good and truly charitable society.

The most severely handicapped people of all may seem to contribute little except their presence, but this is in itself valuable and deserves respect and understanding. Christopher Nickson was a severely mentally and physically handicapped man with a mental age of about eighteen months. When he died at the age of twenty-three his mother said:

> He learned to smile, and when he smiled there was nothing automatic about it. He smiled with his whole being. He was a great asset to society, and gave to all great joy and love.[4]

I will always be grateful that I had the chance to meet Christopher a few years ago. People like him are an important and valuable part of our community. It is unfair on everyone that only the few people who happen to meet them should have the opportunity to learn what they can teach us.

23

People whose contribution to society is emotional, and not economic or academic, are whole, important individuals. By their presence in schools (provided, of course, that the necessary staff and facilities are available) they have an opportunity to make an enormous impact on the spiritual and moral development of able bodied children, as well as contributing to their general education. Ultimately they will also contribute to a fairer, more humane society, where people are valued for themselves, and not merely for their physical strength or measurable 'intelligence'.

It is time we established a completely new approach to disability; maybe indeed a new attitude to people in general and how they should be treated. The practice of categorising and separating handicapped people according to the things they cannot do, carries the tacit assumption that any problems they encounter as people are their personal burdens, rather than the responsibility of the whole community. Education on a human, as well as an academic, level can only be achieved in an atmosphere of tolerance and acceptance of those with disabilities, whatever their cause or degree.

This will demand a degree of openness also on the part of the handicapped, which involves a measure of trust which most of us have sadly concluded cannot be expected of the able bodied. When we trust another person, we make ourselves vulnerable: to ridicule, to rejection, and to damage to our self esteem. Yet it is ultimately the only way for us to be accepted as equals with talents and limitations just like everyone else. We cannot expect people to understand our needs unless we tell them what these are. And, since, as I believe, we are as God made us and intended us to be, there ought to be no embarrassment at explaining exactly what we need. We ought to have the confidence and self assurance to realise that rejection and ridicule are problems of the people doing the rejecting, and not of those of us on the receiving end.

On the part of the able bodied, such a degree of openness and trust would entail a change in perspective. To replace the competitive, ruthless attitude so common in schools, and in adult society, with a truly charitable approach would indeed be revolutionary, yet revolutionary love is at the heart of the Christian faith. We need a radical change of outlook if we are to be educated to regard other people as an integral part of our lives rather than as rivals to be defeated or trampled underfoot. But there is no doubt it would also contribute to a better, more caring, more truly Christian, community.

There is a lesson here for us all – that we cannot claim to be loving, full human beings, and expect others to treat us as such, if at the same time we deny that right to people we see as different or 'less perfect' than ourselves.

Ask yourself

(1) Were there any handicapped people at your school?

(2) If not, do you think it would have been a realistic possibility to include disabled pupils? If not, why?

(3) Do you think it will ever be possible to have mentally handicapped people (with special teachers) in ordinary classes?

(4) Would you want your able bodied children to be in classes with handicapped children?

(5) Would you want segregated or integrated education if you had a disabled child? What if you were yourself disabled?

(6) Do handicapped people need to learn special skills? If so, can this be done in ordinary schools, or only in a more specialised environment?

(7) To what extent do you think concentrating on the disability detracts from a general education?

(8) Is it right to spend taxpayers' money on making ordinary schools accessible to handicapped people? Should all new schools be built with handicapped pupils in mind?

3

Castles in the Air

To have somewhere to live is a basic human need, and according to the United Nations Declaration on Human Rights (Article 25) it is also a universal right. Home should be a place where people are free to be themselves, to relax, to develop and to be secure. 'An Englishman's home is his castle,' the adage assures us; yet for many people with disabilities, having a home of their own seems more like a castle in the air – an impossible dream.

More recently than most of us care to remember, 'the disabled', and especially the mentally handicapped, were shut away in 'defective colonies', preferably in the country behind high walls, so that the rest of society could, and did, conveniently forget about them. We can all recall Hammer Horror films featuring 'The Institution', with creaking trees, thunder, lightning and fog always well in evidence, and a local populace scared out of their wits when one of 'them' escaped. It seems far fetched, yet the reality was in many cases not so very different (timely electrical storms apart!). Some people still have a long way to go before such fear and ignorance are finally laid to rest.

In 1982, for instance, the landlord of a pub in Teignmouth refused to serve a party of mentally handicapped people, and offered their nurse five pounds to take them elsewhere. A television reporter interviewed several residents of the town, who all said that 'of course they were not prejudiced' (I have yet to hear anyone admit that they *are* prejudiced), but they did think such people would be better off 'in the country away from the crowds'. It does not take much imagination to see that what they really wanted to say was that such people should be kept away from 'normal' people. Fortunately the voice of sanity eventually prevailed in the person of Paul Bourge, manager of the Royal Hotel who welcomes handicapped guests and said he believed these people had a right to enjoy the facilities of the town, just the same as non-handicapped guests.

This incident may seem unrelated to the issue of housing, but in fact I think it is central to the whole debate. Unless handicapped people can take their place fully in the community, living, working and relaxing with the able bodied, a ghetto effect takes over with a vengeance.

The Declaration of Human Rights states that everyone has a right not just to housing, but to *adequate* housing. This is sadly far from being a reality for many disabled people in this country, let alone those in poorer parts of the world.

I have travelled extensively during the last few years, and have seen at first hand the kind of deprivation so many people suffer. I have seen people in India living in cardboard boxes and corrugated iron shacks. I have seen whole families living on the pavements, while commuters step over them every morning to get to their air-conditioned offices.

In other parts of Asia and in North Africa I have seen beggars with horrendous, preventable disabilities, who consider me with envy rather than pity because I am rich enough to be able to travel and have a wheelchair. Yet perhaps the saddest people of all are those who are poor and disadvantaged in the midst of plenty. Those in the developed, industrialised West – the richest societies history has ever known – who have inadequate or unsuitable homes, are suffering from negligence, neglect, or simply lack of concern; and this applies not only to disabled people but to anyone who is suffering the appalling handicap of homelessness. It is something no Christian should be prepared to accept.

Unsuitable living accommodation can turn a disabled person into a prisoner in their own home, denied access to the outside world and forced to depend on others. It is literally a living nightmare for a person to be unable to get out of the house without help or, especially for those who are incontinent, to have difficulty getting to a bathroom. I know from bitter experience the feelings of helplessness and shame such frustrations can generate. The whole life of a disabled person can revolve around getting to the toilet in time, and the psychological pressure can be intense. It turns a disability into an unbearable handicap, and can totally distort the personality.

So, as an exercise, try to imagine it. It will be a challenge to your imagination and your empathy, but it is something any able bodied person who wants to really understand must attempt. The format of this mind game is common to many magazine quizzes, except that the aim there is to discover how popular you are, or how socially skilled. Here it is to find out what it feels like to be an incontinent disabled person in an inaccessible house:

You are a paraplegic, incontinent of both bladder and bowel. You have an indwelling catheter and wear a bag to collect urine. You occasionally have diarrhoea, which you are unable to control. One day you are alone in a house which only has an upstairs toilet. The urine bag leaks, and simultaneously you have an attack of diarrhoea (NB This is *not* a hypothetical case!) Do you:

(a) Sit in your wheelchair and stink, trying to put your mind on higher things (or lower, as the case may be), until someone comes? Bear in mind that you will then have to explain to the person who does come, and that people you don't know very well will almost inevitably find such a revelation acutely embarrassing.

(b) Attempt to crawl upstairs, carrying your equipment and a change of clothes (doubtless creating an unspeakable mess on the way)?

(c) Phone the neighbours (who have offered to help if you need it, but almost certainly didn't have this sort of situation in mind)?

(d) Phone a friend or relative who does understand but who will have to drive a few miles, and upset their own timetable?

(e) Cry?

(f) Re-evaluate your need to be in such an inaccessible house at all (relatively easy if you are a visitor, extremely difficult if you live there)?

28

This, of course, is just a game, but it is a game with a purpose. Many disabled people face just such agonising problems every day of their lives. Success in coping is demonstrated by being able to live an ordinary life with a minimum of frustration; failure by psychological damage, loss of self-esteem, maybe loss of job, and of social contacts. As I hope is by now obvious, housing is an issue of crucial importance for anyone with a disability.

The organisation Christian Care for the Mentally Handicapped (Acorn Trust) in its leaflet *From Acorns to Oaks* says:

> To make the right provision for people with a handicap, we must first get our thinking about them right. They are people! They are as interesting and ordinary as that. So the right place for them to be is among other people, in the community. To shove them out on the fringes or into former isolation hospitals – as if they were infectious or dangerous animals is no way to treat these people.

This is, to me, self-evidently true, but unfortunately our country is a very long way from achieving it. The present Conservative government has actually cut the number of accessible accommodation units being built, despite an increased need, and the stock of such units is now only about 10 per cent of what is required.

Homelessness, or inadequate housing, is not a problem most people immediately think of in connection with the disabled, but it is actually an enormous hidden problem. This is especially so for those who would like to leave institutions, or the homes of their parents, but who are unable to see a sensible way of doing so. For instance, a 1986 report by the Royal College of Physicians estimated that over half of physically handicapped people under retirement age in residential care lived in inappropriate places – generally geriatric hospital wards, or old people's homes. Even those in young chronic sick units or locally based hospital units may be only slightly better off, since these are mainly situated in hospital grounds. They also often accommodate older people, despite their brief to cater for the *young* chronic sick and disabled.

The ultimate aim must be for disabled people, like everyone else, to make their own choice about where they want to live, and for most this would naturally be as 'normal' an environment as possible. It is not enough, though, just to move handicapped people out of institutions and assume the problem is thus conveniently solved. Unless they move to suitable accessible accommodation nothing useful is achieved at all.

There are, in any case, plenty of problems in store for handicapped people who want to live in the community, again particularly for those with mental handicaps. Under the 1959 Mental Health Act it is usually still necessary to apply for planning permission for a 'hostel for the mentally disordered' even if it is only going to be slightly bigger than an average household – say perhaps eight mentally handicapped people living with or without help in an ordinary house. This is totally discriminatory, and needs to be changed. If you don't agree, just consider the outcry there would be if eight doctors, or lawyers, had to get permission before being allowed to share a house.

The main obstacle to handicapped people living in the community seems always to be 'opposition from the neighbours', which I am sure is generally simply due to a fear of the unknown. Obviously people who are worried need to be reassured, not least because handicapped tenants are hardly likely to fit easily into a hostile neighbourhood. However, at the end of the day, handicapped people have as much right to live wherever they choose as the able bodied. The fear of a drop in house prices (usually misconceived in any case) is not enough to allow prejudicial attitudes to prevail. Discrimination against handicapped people is no more defensible than racism, and deserves to be treated with the same contempt by all thinking, caring Christians.

Physically handicapped people generally find it slightly (but only slightly) easier to live in the community. The biggest problem here is usually financial; there is a particularly vicious and intractable circle of deprivation to be overcome – poor education and lack of opportunity often lead to unemployment or low-paid jobs, which in turn result in lack of choice over housing. The government's Independent Living Fund, set up to help disabled people pay for the care they need to live in the community, may help considerably, and could make the difference between a normal ordinary life and an institutional existence.

Some national charities have their own housing schemes, which can help establish people in the community, and train them to live independently. I find that able bodied people tend at times to underestimate the amount of physical energy and determination necessary to live independently with a handicap – or maybe it's just something they never think about. So perhaps it's time for another game. This one is in two parts, and you need to participate with your body and your mind.

Try one morning to get dressed without ever standing up or taking weight on your legs. If you are feeling particularly adventurous, you might also try to have a bath! Then have a go at cooking a meal and washing up, sitting down all the time. (Do you get sore arms, because the sink and working surfaces are too high? So do I, every day.)

The second part of the game is more imaginative than phsyical. Imagine that you are too severely handicapped to get yourself up, or cook your own meal. So you have to direct another person to do everything for you. What clothes do you want to wear today (without looking in your wardrobe)? What goes on first? How hot do you like your bath water (without actually being able to feel it first yourself)? What would you want to eat, if you were unable to cut food up for yourself? You may find this a salutary exercise!

It is surprising, though, what can be achieved, given proper advice and training, and also adequate help in the home. Even very severely disabled people, such as those paralysed from the neck down, can live independently in the community, with the help of services such as home helps, district nurses, community service volunteers, etc. There are drawbacks – for instance those who need help to get to bed at night may feel restricted because they never know, even to within a few hours, when their nurses will arrive to put them to bed, so social life can be curtailed. But Stephen Burton, a lawyer with cerebral palsy, who relies on community service volunteers for all his daily living needs, put things in a nutshell when he asserted: 'I am confined to a wheelchair, quite unable to wash, dress or feed myself, but I can still slam my own front door!'[1]

Mentally handicapped people can also enjoy independent and ordinary living either in community houses, or villages like those run by the Camphill Trust. Nigel Hunt, the first person with Down's Syndrome to write a book (*The World of Nigel Hunt*, one of my firm favourites), has lived in a Camphill Village for many years and very much enjoys the community atmosphere. The Home Far Trust also operates self-supporting households, where the work is hard, but the sense of achievement and reward correspondingly great. Mencap run a scheme whereby houses willed to them by supporters are used to create group homes in the community.

Christian Care for the Mentally Handicapped again stands out as an organisation which combines practicality with a positive caring attitude. It was started by Madeleine and David Potter, who were concerned about the future for their own Down's Syndrome daughter. David Potter wrote an article in the *Evangelical Times* in 1973, describing the need for long term care, and suggesting that churches should open homes and run them with the help of a national organisation. Now there are eight such homes, each with long waiting lists.

What is always needed is more money, more resources and more awareness of the needs of handicapped adults. The Bible tells us that we *are* 'our brother's keeper'. It would be a foolhardy Christian who defended inaction by claiming, 'That's nothing to do with me.'

Naturally, some people with disabilities need training to master the considerable skills needed to live independently (some of which you will appreciate more fully if you tried the games earlier in this chapter). I have taught on several such Independence Courses run, among others, by the Spina

Bifida Association, and have thus shared the tremendous feeling of fulfilment when tasks which seemed quite impossible at the beginning of the week become both possible and practical by the end.

It is very often the case that a few simple aids or adaptations will make a house completely accessible. Such obvious things as ramps, lowered surfaces, wider doors and rails for the toilet and bath can help a lot, but they are not magical. The basic requirement for independent living is still the will of the individual and the help society is prepared to offer.

Some disabled people, of course, will never be able to live independently, even with help, and for them the choice may be the simple one of living with their families, or going into a 'home'. The former arrangement tends to be decreasingly satisfactory as the parents get older, and the disabled person heavier or more limited. Carers, be they parents or not, have rights too, and should not be expected to cope with virtually impossible physical or emotional burdens.

The Invalid Care Allowance, payable to carers, is not sufficient, and in any case is not even paid to the most pressurised carers of all – children caring for disabled or ill parents. Many of these youngsters are highly responsible and happy to be of help, but they ought not to be left to cope entirely alone. We are all responsible for each other in a civilised society, and this needs to be recognised, and acted upon.

There is nothing selfish about carers needing a break occasionally, and respite care in a home or with another volunteer family can be extremely helpful. One valuable organisation is the Crossroads Care Scheme. This provides trained temporary carers for disabled people, either on odd occasions when the person who regularly looks after them needs to be away, or on a regular basis – say for one night per week – so that they can sometimes put their own needs first, without worrying and feeling guilty. Many more such facilities are needed. Fortunately I know of several Christian people who are able to provide this kind of help.

Debby and Nigel Hill are one such couple. Their second son, Timothy, was born with microcephaly and lived for only seven months, during which time his life hung in the balance several times. Yet when he died Debby said: 'To list the ways he has enriched my life, leaving behind a legacy too priceless to be valued, would take forever.' Debby and Nigel, with their other son Justin, are now providing respite care for handicapped children, and the children who spend time with them will be very fortunate indeed. No life is ever 'wasted' or 'worthless', however short, and however disabled, something which the story of Timothy Hill, aged seven months and profoundly handicapped, demonstrates very clearly.[2]

Living in 'a home' or an institution need not be regarded as a failure, providing it is what the individual chooses. Paul James Callaghan, for example, who lives in a Cheshire Home, advises other disabled people: 'Do not be afraid of going into a home, because in some cases you can be more independent there than you can be at home.'[3] This may be difficult to accept for those disabled who are able to live in the community. While I fully agree with the politically active groups, such as the Union of the Physically Impaired Against Segregation, who regard enforced institutionalisation as a kind of apartheid, for some it may be the best option; providing always that it is what they choose for themselves.

Ultimately, I suppose, the inter-related issues of housing, employment and education come down to a very basic point: that all people should be given the maximum opportunity to develop their full potential, and to contribute to a share in the life of their communities.

James Agee writes in his book *Let Us Now Praise Famous Men*:

> I believe that every human being is potentially capable, within his limits, of fully realising his potentialities; and that his being cheated and choked of it is infinitely the ghastliest, commonest, and most inclusive of all the crimes of which the human world can accuse itself.

This epitomises what has happened to people with disabilities in the past. It is up to us all to see that the future is different.

Ask yourself

(1) Could a person in a wheelchair come to your house as a guest a) at all? b) without feeling embarrassed or self-conscious?

(2) How far would you be prepared to go to make your house accessible if you had a disabled friend or family member?

(3) To what extent do you think concessions to accessibility should outweigh aesthetic considerations (e.g. should historic and beautiful staircases be knocked down to build ramps)?

(4) Would you mind living next door to a group of mentally handicapped people? Be honest. If you would be uneasy about it, try to work out why. If it is simply fear, have you ever really known any mentally handicapped people?

(5) Could you contemplate providing occasional respite care of disabled or elderly neighbours, to give their regular carers a break?

(6) If you became handicapped, how would you want the neighbours to react? And where would you want to live?

4

Jobs for the Boys?

Over the last ten years or so I have noticed that whenever unemployment is under discussion it is always the figures for 'able bodied men out of work' which are quoted. This says a lot about our society's attitude to the handicapped, to women, and to the nature of employment itself.

I am talking here about 'employment' in its widest possible sense, including not only paid, full time work (which is what most people mean by the word) but also the alternatives to it – part time work, community work, sheltered workshops, training centres, and what would more generally be termed occupational therapy. It is also important to remember that severely handicapped people can create employment for others, for this is part of what the 'caring professions' are all about.

Work is such an integral part of most people's lives that even in the present climate of high unemployment, 'How do you earn your living?' is one of the first questions we tend to ask a new acquaintance. It is almost as if we need to know that before we can really begin to relate to the person; as if what they do helps us to define who they are. This is quite understandable when we remember that work, in one form or another, occupies the greater part of most people's lives.

Those who are not gainfully employed often feel a sense of failure or uselessness, or that they are in some way inferior, because they don't 'hold down a job'. This is true for most unemployed people, but for the disabled, being rejected for work can be a particularly bitter blow; yet another example of rejection or discrimination.

Unemployment ratios for the physically handicapped are about double those for the able bodied, and the mentally handicapped are generally even worse off. Recent figures[1] showed that 26 per cent of disabled job seekers had been out of work for over two years, compared with only 8 per cent of the non-disabled.

The reasons why disabled people are so disadvantaged in employment are diverse, but eventually it comes back to the same problem every time – lack of understanding by the able bodied community, and the misconception that disability equals inability.

What happened to me after leaving university was probably fairly typical. I applied for about fifty jobs, stating that I was confined to a wheelchair, but otherwise quite fit and able to work. Back came the replies, with the most amazing collection of reasons for not employing me. I was too old, or too young, too well qualified or not qualified enough. I had too little experience, or too much. The workplace was inaccessible, or they felt I would not 'fit in' (having never met me, of course). Some didn't even bother to offer an excuse but just stated that the position had been filled.

Deciding that this was getting beyond a joke, I went to visit the Disablement Resettlement Officer at the local Job-centre. Surely he would understand the problem, I thought, and give me some help and advice. Maybe he would have done, if I had ever managed to see him. When I arrived at the Jobcentre, I was told that his office was at the top of a flight of stairs, and that there was no lift!

We could perhaps excuse employers for being ignorant, or afraid of disability, and for consciously or unconsciously discriminating about conditions they know nothing about. But what excuse could there possibly be for the Disablement Resettlement Officer? I could only conclude that he, like many other people, held the erroneous and naive view that if you can't walk, you can't work.

The problems disabled people face in getting open employment are probably very similar to those of any minority group wanting to do ordinary things that are not generally expected of them. Women wanting to do construction jobs, for instance, or black people wanting to be lawyers. Maybe also even daughters of manual labourers who want to be doctors or physicists. The instinctive reaction of mainstream society to all of these ambitions seems to be 'Whatever gives you the idea you could do that?' or 'Why on earth would you want to do that?' or, more damningly, 'Someone like you couldn't possibly do that!' There is a hidden wealth of talent waiting to be used, of people who want to work, and could do so. This needs to be recognised. It is not good enough just to count the 'able bodied men'. We ought to be concerned about everyone who wants to work, but is prevented from doing so.

I have a friend who has a deformed arm, who applied for a job as a hospital domestic, only to be told that she could not do the work. How did her prospective employers know this? They would not allow her to demonstrate, but were content instead to trust their own preconceptions, which were in fact wrong. In this case there was a happy ending. She now works in a day centre for mentally handicapped adults, in a job which is rewarding and challenging, and interestingly enough far more physically demanding than being a hospital domestic. She succeeded because finally an employer was prepared to be imaginative and to recognise her abilities rather than her disability. If only more would follow this example.

Anyone with a disability knows only too well this vexing problem of confronting what other people think we can and can't do. This is something Christians in particular should be aware of, for it manifests itself even in the Church. Alyn Haskey, who has cerebral palsy and is currently a lay reader in the Church of England told me:

Whilst at theological college I had an interview with the suffragan bishop. It was a very friendly time and at the end he seemed quite sure that all would go well. It was only afterwards that I discovered he had done a complete turn around in the course of our meeting. Apparently on his arrival he had said that in no way could I be a lay reader.

Later, however, Alyn experienced difficulties, and the only answer he could get out of his parish rector was that lay readership was 'not appropriate' for him. He explains:

The only concession was that I might occasionally be

allowed to preach in church. There was no way to appeal, no one I could challenge. The only thing left open to me was to question how one bishop could say yes and another no. The next two years were hard and painful. What do you do when you know you have a ministry, when God tells you you have, but the Church doesn't want to know? I spent most of my time reminding people that I was available and writing letters applying for jobs. In all cases the replies were much the same – kind wishes but nothing positive.[2]

Alyn now has the status of a 'commended evangelist' but still finds it very hard to get invitations to speak. He would like eventually to be ordained, but obviously there are many problems to be overcome first, mainly it seems in the attitude of the Church to a disabled person having a ministry.

This problem of bias and ignorance is our first and greatest hurdle in applying for employment. If only we can make a prospective employer understand that it would be possible for us to do the job, we at least have a good chance of persuading him to give it a try.

This can best be achieved by a combination of different approaches. First, and crucially, the law needs to be enforced. Firms employing more than twenty people have a legal obligation to include disabled people as at least 3 per cent of their workforce; yet hardly any comply with this requirement. This may arise from unwillingness to adapt the premises or the particular job, rather than from calculated prejudice; but grants are available from the Manpower Services Commission to make it possible for disabled people to be given jobs.

In West Germany there are effective financial penalties for firms who fail to employ the disabled, and the fines are used to subsidise those who do. Good will is not enough to combat prejudice and discrimination. There have to be sound policies too.

Our task of making able bodied employers and workers aware of what we can do, rather than concentrating on what we cannot do, would be a lot easier if trade unions were more sympathetic to the needs of disabled people. Active trade unionists may feel that this criticism is unfair, since many unions do take an interest in the welfare of disabled workers – NALGO, for instance, have established a national committee to identify the needs of disabled members, and have published a *Guide to Negotiating on Behalf of Disabled Workers*.

At the same time, however, this same union, typical of many, has also been extremely vociferous in defending 'a woman's right to choose' on abortion, particularly highlighting the 'need' for abortion if the baby is found to be handicapped. This kind of inconsistency is both unjust and uncaring; you cannot claim to have a positive attitude to disabled people if at the same time you campaign for better facilities to enable them to be eliminated before birth.

It is time, I think, for trade unionists to face a fundamental truth. Human rights only have meaning if they apply equally to everyone. The United Nations Declaration on Human Rights (Article 23) states that: 'Everyone has the right to work and to free choice of employment, and to just and favourable conditions of work.' In order to claim this right, of course, one must first secure the most basic human right of all – the right to life.

It was after the Second World War, when disabled people had had an unprecedented opportunity to prove themselves capable of work, that open employment began to be a real possibility. Employers who had actually given disabled people a chance almost always found that they were just as capable as anyone else, and in many cases were more conscientious than average, proving that discrimination on the grounds of handicap simply didn't make sense.

But what about people who cannot compete for open employment? Some cannot yet do so, some will never be able to do so; and it is very important to realise that this is not a failure to live up to 'normality' but simply a recognition that something different is needed.

There are several schemes which can help provide alternatives, one of which is the Share Community, which was set up by Tom Hood. Disabled in the Second World War, he experienced at first hand the frustrations common to many disabled people. He went through intensive therapy in' hospital, rehabilitation and training for work, and then after all that suffered the soul-destroying rejection of unemployment. He was a Quaker, which is why that society has supported the work of Share ever since.

Share projects provide temporary employment and work skill training to discover what each person can do best. They accept people with varying disabilities, and offer experience at such jobs as clerical and management work, computer operating and programming and printing.

In the past disabled people who did manage to get work often ended up in unskilled jobs with poor pay and prospects, generally because their education and training had been inadequate. This was especially true of the mentally handicapped and those who had attended special schools, who generally spent their working lives doing dull, repetitive or downright useless tasks. It is time for this to be changed, not least because so many are capable of doing much more.

The Disablement Income Group has run a campaign for many years to achieve a working wage for those able to work, and a suitable level of income support for those who cannot. The need is quite apparent: some handicapped people, particularly those who attend Adult Training Centres, work a full week, and only get pocket money because they are not considered 'profitable'. This is patently unfair. Both they and those unable to work at all are equally entitled to a decent standard of living.

For people who could work, but need some help in getting started, Pathway, an employment service run by Mencap, has proved very helpful. The benefits have not only been one-way either; after taking on a mentally handicapped person, often with more than a little trepidation, many employers have returned to Pathway asking for more. The reasons they cite for doing so include the comments that they find their mentally handicapped employees punctual, hard working and very conscientious – qualities which are not too common these days among able bodied workers!

Handicapped people often have firm ideas about what they want to do, an initiative which should be nurtured, not squashed and extinguished. Sarah Duffen is a good example of what this can mean.

Sarah is twenty-one and was the first person with Down's Syndrome to pass the driving test. She said of this achievement: 'I hope I have pushed forward the frontiers for others like me.' Sarah could read by the age of five, and is now using a home computer to complete her education. She is also thinking of setting up her own pie making business. Competitive employment is not the only way in which people with disabilities can make their mark. But Sarah's example shows that for some it is an exciting, rewarding and entirely realistic possibility.[3]

Like Sarah, after all the problems and rejections, I succeeded in finding work which is worthwhile and rewarding. Indeed, I do not think there is anything more worth doing than protecting the lives of my fellow human beings. I work mostly from home, but I also travel around the world, speaking on the right to life of handicapped people. From time to time I also go into the offices of the Society for the Protection of Unborn Children, whose Handicap Division I run. The office is situated on the fourth floor of a building with no lift, but the goodwill (and muscles!) of my colleagues overcome that obstacle. All of which goes to prove that the things handicapped people really 'cannot do', given encouragement and support, are very few indeed.

It is important to bear in mind that employment does not only provide an income. It also fosters a sense of self worth and achievement, and provides a time structure to the day, colleagues and friends, and a purpose in life. But the feeling of doing something of value is not confined only to those in conventional full time work.

Employment in its widest sense means how we use our time to contribute to society and to develop as people, and this can be done in many different ways – in an office, a school, a hospital, a factory, a sheltered workshop, a supermarket, an Adult Training Centre, or at home. It is not the sole preserve of any one environment, but could more correctly be described as a particular frame of mind.

Day Centres and Adult Training Centres can either be 'dumping grounds' for severely handicapped people, or real opportunities for training and occupying those who attend. As ever, it depends entirely on the attitudes and degree of enlightenment of the people involved. Almost all people with disabilities are capable of being 'employed' in some way, even if that simply means learning to appreciate the presence of another person, laughing, moving, eating. The most severely handicapped of all create employment for others, be they parents or care staff, but they themselves are also employed – in learning about themselves and others, and the world they inhabit. Perhaps education and employment are always interconnected, but in this case they are one and the same thing.

Bernadette Nolan, a nurse in a special hospital for severely handicapped people explained to me more fully what this means in practice:

> I know from experience that in such a home the residents are picked up and hugged, and many develop an affectionate relationship with their nurses. The work is hard, but when someone described as 'hopeless' takes for the first time a few tottering steps, or holds his own spoon to feed himself, the feeling of reward for him and us is terrific.

This feeling of achievement is just as important as the concrete end-product of a conventional job, and can be got in many different ways. Some disabled people can work in ordinary jobs, others need sheltered environments such as that provided by Remploy. Some can live in villages, such as those at Papworth or Enham, where whole families, handicapped and able bodied, live and work together. Others can take part in Community Programmes, and become involved very deeply in different projects. A few have high profile jobs in the media, and entertainment. A comedian with cerebral palsy appeared on television on 'Friday Night Live', and succeeded in three minutes in banishing stereotypes that have been prevalent for hundreds of years.

The most vital, worthwhile job any human being can do is to interact with other people and help them to grow and develop a caring attitude. Paradoxically it is sometimes the most severely handicapped of all who come closest to achieving this.

Ask yourself

(1) Are there any handicapped people at your place of work?

(2) What problems would a person in a wheelchair encounter at your workplace? Could it be made accessible?

(3) Consider if there are any jobs you think handicapped people could never do.

(4) Do you agree with the quota system? If not, how could it be replaced with a more workable system?

(5) Is sheltered employment a form of positive discrimination, or just a form of ghettoisation?

5

Getting There?

'The fortunes of men are all bound together, and it is impossible to inflict damage without receiving it.' So said the *Bhagavad Gita*, the masterpiece of Sanskrit literature written 500 years BC. I believe it is as true and relevant now as it was then. To use the term 'inflicting damage' as applied to denying access for the disabled may seem rather an exaggeration, but that is how it often feels for us on the receiving end. The problems are not always deliberately imposed (although they sometimes are), but it is certainly fair to say that they do exist.

I would indeed be a wealthy woman if I had a pound for every time I have been invited to a house or a meeting venue with the bland assurance that 'of course' it is accessible, to find on arrival that there are steps up to the door. This is made even more frustrating if, as often happens, the door-bell is out of reach, so there is no way to announce my presence. More depressing still is to accept an invitation to stay with someone who has an 'accessible' house, only to find that the bathroom and toilet are upstairs.

Such incidents are salutary for both parties, but at least both can learn from them: the able bodied person that disabled people have to perform natural functions too, and the disabled that we cannot expect to have our requirements anticipated unless we are explicit about what we need. My own problem with this is just that I often forget that I am 'severely disabled', because my condition is so very ordinary to me. I think this is a fairly healthy 'fault' but it can undoubtedly sometimes put me in rather awkward situations.

Lack of access due to misunderstanding is one thing. Deliberate discrimination is another. And contrary to popular belief there is still an unacceptable level of this prevalent in society. If we were discriminated against every minute of every day, maybe we could work out good strategies for coping with it. It is the continuous uncertainty that can really damage self confidence and self esteem, and make life unnecessarily hazardous. (I am sure that many black people suffer the same experience, and will identify with this very closely.)

Perhaps another game will best illustrate what I mean.

Suppose you are a normal able bodied person who was born with bright orange hair. You consider yourself (quite rightly) to be just an ordinary human being. Your colouring does have a few practical drawbacks – for instance you get burned if you stay out in the sun too long. But you can handle that, so what is the problem? The problem is other people, who think it is 'abnormal' to be born with orange hair. They tell you how brave and courageous you are; how they can't imagine *how* you stay so cheerful, having 'that' colour hair.

When you go out people usually tolerate your presence, though you often have to explain to the curious what it feels like to have orange hair. (This is difficult for you, because you have never experienced *not* having orange hair!) You also have to phone ahead every time you plan a trip to the cinema or theatre, or when you want to use public transport, just to ensure nobody will mind. Why on earth should they? You are, after all an ordinary average adult. Yet experience has taught you that, inexplicable though it seems, other people think of you as being substantially different, and so put barriers in your way.

As a result of this you have always been segregated to a certain extent. There are special schools and workshops and homes for the orange haired, and it is very difficult to break out of the system and live in ordinary communities. Sometimes there are adverts in the newspapers or on television to raise money for people like you, who on the one hand are portrayed as 'an inspiration' and on the other are regarded as better not born at all. Occasionally you are barred from places of entertainment because the management says orange haired people upset the other customers.

Do you think this is far fetched? Read on!

In 1988 I travelled to Australia to do a Pro-life speaking tour. I flew to Perth by British Airways, then on to Adelaide, Launceston, Hobart, Sydney and Canberra by Ansett Airlines, then home again by Qantas. When booking the ticket I explained about my disability, which is static and not deteriorating. I can cope with my physical needs by myself on planes. A narrow-aisle wheelchair is useful, so that I can get to the toilet with some degree of dignity, but if the airline cannot provide one then I crawl. People do stare, which is unpleasant, but if the only alternative is to stay at home, so be it.

One would think it would be enough that I explain my needs and answer any questions which might arise, but no. My doctor was sent long forms by each airline, on which he was asked to describe my disability and its effects. Each one ended with a declaration certifying that my 'disease' was not contagious, and that I would not be 'distressing, inconvenient or embarrassing' to the other passengers. Able bodied people are never asked such things, even though, I maintain, some of them are much more likely to distress or embarrass others than I am. My only choice, however, was to get the form filled in, or not go.

Another interesting fact I have discovered about travelling by plane, is that people with disabilities are not generally allowed to sit nearest the door, even though that would be the most convenient seat to get to. The reason is that in an emergency the crews of most major airlines have explicit instructions to leave disabled people and get the able bodied passengers out first.

Trains are somewhat better, but by no means perfect. Fortunately things are improving slowly; on certain lines, British Rail will take a seat out of a first class carriage to provide easy access for a person in a wheelchair plus one companion. The two main drawbacks with this are,   a) (as ever) the inaccessible toilet, and   b) what to do if you are travelling with more than one other person (say a couple with children).

On some rail lines, however, even these facilities are not yet available, which means that people in wheelchairs have to travel in the guard's van along with the letters and parcels and luggage. It is unheated, which is no joke in winter, draughty and isolated; and of course there is absolutely no way of getting to the toilet. I have spent many a long hour in guards' vans, trying sometimes to read and turn the pages of my book while wearing several pairs of gloves at once. I still have to do it when travelling to London by train from my home in Dorset. I do honestly believe that British Rail are trying hard, as far as disabled people are concerned, to fulfill their vaunted promise of 'getting there'. I just hope it happens soon.

Cars are obviously the easiest mode of transport for most disabled people, and the way the environment has been transformed to facilitate driving just goes to show what can be done when the right incentive is present. I have a car, leased under the government's Motability scheme, which is fitted with hand controls, and though there are some problems (for instance self-service petrol stations), I would hate to be without it.

For those who are unable to drive, getting in and out of standard taxi cabs can be something of an athletic feat; yet in Adelaide, Australia I used adapted 'access cabs' several times. I wish the British version, due to have been introduced in 1986, would make an appearance, since it would make things so much easier. It is quite exhilarating when I find anticipated problems just don't materialise – like the Adelaide taxis, and unexpectedly accessible ferries in Scandinavia. It is such an unusual experience to be 'ordinary' occasionally. The Scandinavian ferries were a particularly pleasant surprise, after trying to manoeuvre a wheelchair on British ferries with their high 'port hole' thresholds around all the doors. I have often been assured by staff on these ferries that such barriers are essential on board ship. In that case, why don't the Scandinavian ships need them? It is obviously technically possible. What are they waiting for?

Sometimes surprising things can be accomplished even in the absence of special facilities, given imagination and maybe an element of daring. A few years ago I travelled around the south of India by train. It was quite an experience. As anyone who knows Indian trains will verify it is interesting, exciting, frightening, boring, annoying and frustrating all at once. It particularly demanded ingenuity on my part, but at least I was never told, as I am so depressingly often here, 'People like you are not allowed to . . .' By dint of a lot of physical exertion and also goodwill (and inevitably in India a lot of curiosity) on the part of my fellow travellers, I managed well.

How very different things often are here. On arriving back at Heathrow I was prevented from using the lift down to the Underground – which, ironically enough, was opened by Princess Anne to commemorate the International Year of Disabled People in 1981. The ticket collector told me I could only use the lift if I could walk (when presumably I would not have actually needed it!) I told him I had come that way on the outward journey. He accused me of lying. I feel myself tense up again even as I write this. Why do people have to be so unfair and stupid and insensitive? Can't they see I'm just like them – a human being with feelings? Perhaps they can't. Perhaps they will only understand if I tell them. Or if you tell them . . .

Nothing ever seems simple or straightforward if you are disabled. Even travel insurance is often discriminatory: some policies will not cover you at all, for anything, even your luggage, if you have a 'pre-existing disability'. Life insurance and motor insurance can be equally problematical. Fortunately things have improved slowly in recent years, but there is still a long way to go before we can start to take such things for granted.

Going out in the evening ought to be a relaxing, enjoyable experience for everyone, and usually I find it so. Most of the time physically disabled people are accepted in pubs, though there are some notable exceptions, as we shall see later. Going to the cinema or theatre, however, is never without hassles, and I very rarely even try. Life is just too short for the kind of complications these expeditions entail.

The 1985 Home Office guidelines on cinema safety stipulated that people in wheelchairs and the blind should never be allowed into cinemas unaccompanied. Wheelchair bound people who cannot transfer to an ordinary seat are generally excluded altogether as being a 'fire risk' – almost as if we were liable to spontaneous combustion! I suppose it really means that such people would be difficult to get out in the event of a fire; but then so would children and elderly people, who are not excluded. It is in any case the buildings that are hazardous to safety, not disabled people.

We are frequently told that this kind of ban is 'for our own safety'. But we need to be allowed to take risks, particularly minimal ones like this, just like everyone else. 'Normal' people can choose to do any number of dangerous things – like hang gliding, or smoking in public, both of which are potentially harmful to themselves or others. The risk of cinema fires is much less than that of injury or damage due to hang gliding or smoking, and we all ought to be able to choose for ourselves whether that risk is acceptable.

To some extent, I think, restrictions like these enable society in general to opt out of its responsibilities. The 1970 Chronically Sick and Disabled Persons Act lays down that access to new buildings should be provided '. . . in so far as it is in the circumstances both practical and reasonable.' Unfortunately, since then almost any reason seems to have been accepted as sufficient to avoid complying with this requirement; and even new amendments to make provision obligatory in some cases have not been enforced. To some extent it is the architects who now hold the key to integration for future generations. In his book *Designing for the Disabled*, Selwyn Goldsmith comments that 'you can never evaluate the material returns of access facilities.' What you can know, is that disabled people have been given a new and unprecedented opportunity to be 'ordinary'.

From time to time I have managed to find cinemas which will admit me, but even then there are almost always special arrangements to be made. The same is true of staying in hotels, or even going out for a meal. It is quite common in these circumstances to be faced with a barrage of daunting conditions such as: 'Not unless you give at least three days' notice'; 'Not if you are unaccompanied'; 'Not at busy times'; 'Not with a guide dog'; 'Only on Tuesdays between two and four.' Special arrangements are all very well for special occasions; but should we really have to spend our whole lives doing a kind of public relations exercise?

A recent survey undertaken by the Paediatric Research Unit of the Royal Devon and Exeter Hospital found that 30 per cent of disabled teenagers never went out socially with friends, compared with 3 per cent of able bodied people. I can quite understand why, and given all the problems encountered, I think it's surprising the proportion is that low.

Maybe by now you think I am exaggerating just a little, being bitter, or painting an unjustly gloomy picture. Let me give a few actual examples.

Anne Wilson, who is confined to a wheelchair, phoned a certain night club to ask if she should be allowed in. They assured her she would, but when she got there a bouncer told her. 'No chance. You can't come in with that thing. It's for your own good, love.' I'm not quite sure how he worked out that it was good for her to be discriminated against, but I am positive that I don't agree.

Nothing daunted, Anne went on to a disco. The bouncer there said, 'You can't come in here. It's members only.' Which is a lie.[1]

A group of deaf people were turned out of a pub because the landlord said their use of sign language was 'upsetting the other customers'.[2]

Disabled residents of a Cheshire Home were asked to leave an inn in Sussex by 8.30, so their wheelchairs would not 'get in the way' at busy times.[3]

Three people in wheelchairs were turned away from a Buckinghamshire pub. The landlord said there was 'No room', even though there were only two customers at the bar. A spokesman explained, 'We would have allowed one of the wheelchairs in' (note how he ignores the fact that it was the people, not the wheelchairs, who wanted to go in), 'but not all three.'[4]

Heard enough? Yet I have hardly started.

The experiences of able bodied people who have tried being in a wheelchair for a day highlight very well the extent to which obstacles face us at every turn. This comes as quite a revelation to the uninitiated. The experience of being pushed, and therefore being to some extent out of control, can in itself be alarming, especially when the chair is tipped back to get up kerbs. The difficulties posed by swing doors, high counters in shops and banks (where at times the assistants don't even realise you are there), deep pile carpets, having to balance shopping bags on the knees while pushing yourself at the same time, all are outside the experience of most people. There is also the ever present problem of finding accessible toilets which are not locked, resulting in sometimes having to restrict fluid intake which is both uncomfortable and unhealthy. (I apologise for continuing to harp on a somewhat unsavoury topic, but we are, after all, talking about a basic human need.)

Well-meaning offers of assistance from members of the public can also have their hazards. Annabel Dean, who used a wheelchair for a day in Sydney, Australia, recounts an all-too-common event in graphic and amusing detail:

> A man pulled my chair out of the car and stuffed me in it before I had a chance to explain anything. When I started to protest that he was doing it all wrong, he didn't hear. 'Don't worry about it, I'm a Christian,' he said.[5]

Unfortunately, meaning well and actually doing some good are not always the same thing!

Undoubtedly, the fact is that most people get embarrassed or anxious in unfamiliar situations, and dealing with the disabled is not a common experience for most. If more handicapped people were seen around in everyday life, and shown in the media doing ordinary things, it would help. Sadly, disabled people are almost always stereotyped in newspaper stories and on TV, as 'tragic victims' or brave cheerful cardboard cutouts. Some charities compound this attitude by stressing the helplessness of the disabled in order to get more money by evoking pity. There have, though, been a few really excellent advertisements in recent years. The Spastics Society, for instance, produced one showing a bride and groom, both in wheelchairs, with the caption, 'When they said John and Mary should be in an institution, they didn't mean this one.' Another depicted a man in a wheelchair at the top of a flight of steps leading down to a toilet saying, 'As far as I'm concerned, it's neither public nor convenient.' My favourite, however, was a poster showing a very attractive little boy with the comments: 'You say Mongol, we say Down's Syndrome, his mates call him David.' In my opinion, this really does say it all.

The National Union of Journalists made a real contribution to encouraging this kind of common sense with their 'Campaign for Real People', which pointed out that disability should only be mentioned if it is actually relevant, and then it should be portrayed in clear, non-emotive language. If this was put into practice on a wider scale, I might get fewer stares and pats on the head from total strangers – the type who usually insist on talking to the person with me and saying cringe-inducing things like 'Isn't she wonderful!'

Something most people simply do not know is that it is not illegal to discriminate against disabled people. There have been several attempts to change this, but to date they have always been unsuccessful. The last Bill, introduced by Robert Wareing MP, failed owing to pressure from the government. They maintained that there was insufficient evidence of discrimination (obviously they did not test this theory by actually trying using a wheelchair for a day!) and that there was in any case a wealth of 'warm good will' towards the disabled in this country. If this is good will, I think I'd prefer bad feeling.

It is only *unjustifiable* discrimination that needs to be outlawed, of course; but in any case I don't think disabled people are particularly unrealistic in their aspirations. I'm not, for instance, suggesting that I could be a steeplejack, if only anti-discrimination legislation were passed. I know I could not do it. Equally well, though, I could not be an accountant, because I am hopeless at arithmetic; neither could I be an interpreter, as I am quite spectacularly slow at languages. The point is that I am just as capable as the able bodied of assessing what I can and cannot do. Disability brings problems enough, without having to fight against deliberately imposed obstacles as well. Martin Luther King once said, 'Morality cannot be legislated, but behaviour can be regulated. Judicial decrees may not change the heart, but they can restrict the heartless.'[6] I agree, and in my opinion the right of disabled people to equal treatment should be enshrined in law.

Every time a disabled person meets with discriminatory attitudes it says something very clearly about the way we are regarded by able bodied society. Every time an accessible toilet is kept locked (with the key held in the Ladies – up two steps – or at the Town Hall, five miles away); every time we are barred from a pub, club, cinema or theatre, or a stately home ('because your wheelchair might mark the carpet'); every time unnecessary restrictions are imposed, or we have to 'go around the back and use the goods lift'; every time someone has to certify that we won't be 'distressing or embarrassing'; the message we get is that we are inferior, and only tolerated on sufferance.

It is not unusual to see notices, especially at exhibitions stating that 'wheelchairs and dogs are not admitted' – which categorises us as definitely less than fully human. Thoughtless and hurtful treatment can make us feel the same way, as happened to me one painfully memorable day. I turned up at the Greenwood Theatre, to take part in a TV programme to which I had been specifically invited, only to be told by the doorman, 'This place was built before people like you were let out. You can't come in.'

Sometimes, though, the excuses get so ludicrous as to be funny. The Committee on Restrictions against Disabled People (CORAD) reported such a case: a Butlin's Holiday Camp which was apparently too hilly for disabled people in the summer, although they could be accommodated in April, May or October. How stupid do they think we are? It's enough to make you wonder who is really handicapped!

Fortunately there are some good things happening now. The Tara Hotel in London has completely accessible rooms at reasonable rates for disabled people, which is very helpful since previously there were only about forty rooms out of 150,000 in London which people in wheelchairs could use. The publication *City Limits* now indicates accessibility for all its cinema and theatre listings, including induction loops for those with hearing impairments. And the political parties are at last beginning to acknowledge our existence. It is also being recognised that disabled people like to participate in sporting activities as well as just watching; something of which I wish the media would take note. In the USA, wheelchair basketball is popular on television, and it would be a great step forward if it could be shown here – not just on programmes about disability, but as a general interest sport.

So what relevance does all this have for the Christian churches, who need more than ever to demonstrate that they have no prejudices against the disabled? My first suggestion is very basic, but perhaps not completely obvious until it is pointed out. It really is not possible to have a positive, humanitarian attitude to us unless you unequivocally support the struggle to secure our equal right to life. It makes no sense at all to say, as many people do, 'I'm not in favour of discrimination against the disabled, but I think pre-natal screening and selective abortion must be available.' If you are ambivalent about killing someone because they would grow up to be like me, how can you regard me as equal to you?

Disabled people need to be accepted by Christians just as they are. Of course there may be physical problems of access in some churches, and naturally people might be embarrassed at first and unsure how to approach the subject. Making the effort is the important thing, but sadly some Christians don't seem even to try to understand. One Sunday I went, with my parents who were staying with me at the time, to a certain Methodist chapel. My father went in first to see if it was accessible for me, and asked the lay preacher there if it would be all right to bring me in. 'No, I don't think there will be room,' he said. My father replied that we would try anyway, and we got in with no difficulty. The congregation that night consisted of my parents, myself, and three others!

Something else we definitely do not need is the well meaning 'spiritual' advice of those who see our disability as something evil to be overcome. Soon after I became a Christian, I was told by a group of fellow Christians that 'If only you have faith enough, God will cure your spina bifida.' It was extremely demoralising at the time, and is an attitude I have frequently encountered since. I want to say to such people: 'How do you know that it is God's will for me to be miraculously cured here and now? How do you know there isn't a good reason for me being as I am? In any case, being cured of spina bifida is not among my first priorities. Why can't you listen to me, and believe me when I say that I want other things more than physical healing – like the gifts of wisdom and compassion?'

The Church should be a gathering of *all* God's people, acknowledging, as Martin Luther King observed that 'We aren't loved because we are beautiful. We are beautiful because we are loved.' This includes the whole spectrum of human shape and intellect, hidden disabilities, hang-ups, phobias – everything that has a human form. Weakness and disability can, after all, be creative – they show that suffering can be borne without loss of human worth and dignity. Those who are able bodied should not deny themselves the lessons people with disabilities can teach; lessons made so clear by St Paul, recounting his own experiences, in 2 Corinthians 12.7–10 (NIV):

> To keep me from becoming conceited because of these surpassingly great revelations, there was given me a thorn in my flesh, a messenger of Satan, to torment me. Three times I pleaded with the Lord to take it away from me. But he said to me, 'My grace is sufficient for you, for my power is made perfect in weakness.' Therefore I will boast all the more gladly about my weaknesses, so that Christ's power may rest on me. That is why, for Christ's sake, I delight in weaknesses, in insults, in hardships, in persecutions, in difficulties. For when I am weak, then I am strong.

Ask yourself

(1) Does your church include any disabled people? If not, how would you welcome someone with a disability attending for the first time?

(2) Do you think people with disabilities should be allowed equal access to places of entertainment, public buildings and

transport? Would you be prepared to take some action (e.g. writing to the newspapers) if you discovered this was not happening?

(3) Why do you think disabled people suffer discrimination? Is legislation the answer? If not, what is the answer?

(4) Think of the route you take to get to work, or to church, or to go out in the evening. Could a disabled person easily do it?

(5) How many disabled people do you think would have to visit a particular place in order to justify making it accessible? (But bear in mind that until it is accessible disabled people will be put off from using it!)

(6) How could public transport systems be made more accessible?

6

See what I Mean?

Communication is the basis of all human interaction. It is necessary for all of us to explain our needs and desires, our likes and dislikes, our feelings, emotions and thoughts – in fact to establish our own unique and distinct personality.

Communication with other people is essential to all except perhaps those very few who choose to forgo the privilege and live as hermits. It encompasses not just talking, but also the whole complicated language of body movements – smiles, grimaces, eye contact, gestures, signals. These are heavily culturally based, and differ just as much as spoken language, if rather more subtly. I found communicating with people in some parts of India confusing to say the least until I realised that a shake of the head meant 'yes'. Equally problematical, though in a different way, was the realisation that in some areas of North Africa, it is the number of fingers *not* held up which denotes 'how many'.

For many handicapped people, communication is the biggest and most intractable problem, for it is only when we can communicate effectively that we can influence the human society of which we are a part. Everyone knows the story of Helen Keller, who became blind and deaf at the age of eighteen months, and was subsequently taught by Annie Sullivan, who was herself partially sighted. The young Helen was an unruly child, totally beyond the control of her family. Indeed, at one point her uncle advised putting her into an institution, declaring that she was mentally retarded and 'ugly to behold'.

Annie Sullivan taught Helen the power of language as a communication tool, and finally succeeded in persuading her that signs and objects are connected, and that 'everything has a name'. Annie graphically summed up the important role of communication:

Language grows out of life, out of its needs and experiences. I never taught language for its own sake, but invariably used it as a medium for the communication of thought. Thus the learning of language was coincident with the acquisition of knowledge.

The hardest thing for anyone to bear is surely the burden of the incommunicable. This has relevance both to people like me, who need to explain that we do not need always to be regarded as 'special', and also to those whose communication problem is more immediate and more basic.

Most profoundly deaf people experience overwhelming difficulties with communication. It is not so much that they are incapable of communicating, but that the able bodied community is, by and large, unable to understand their language. Obviously it is a basic necessity of proper communication that both the transmitter and the receiver of information must understand the same language, whether it is verbal or not, and if everyone understood signing it would help the integration of many deaf people.

It is, however, completely unrealistic to expect hearing people to spend years perfecting a knowledge of sign language, when they may never meet a deaf person who uses it (some deaf people, for instance, rely solely on lipreading). But I do suggest that it would be a good idea for every child to be taught finger spelling at school. Most people can grasp it in about half an hour, and it permits at least basic communication with the profoundly deaf. Even people who generally use lipreading find some words hard, or even impossible to make out (some letters look exactly the same on the lips – try saying 'B' and 'P' in a mirror), so finger spelling can occasionally be helpful for them too.

British Sign Language is a complete language in itself, and actually very enjoyable and interesting to learn if you have time. There is also a simplified form called Makaton, which is taught to mentally handicapped people, and has enabled many to communicate their needs quickly and effectively for the first time.

The Breakthrough Trust, which was formed to break down barriers between the hearing and the deaf has had considerable success, and I'm sure most hearing people are only too glad to be told how they can best help. Finger spelling is a good start; and you will find the two handed system, used in the UK and Australia, at the end of this book. Give it a try!

The most important thing, again, is making the effort, and realising that handicapped people have things worth saying too. There is no good reason at all for regarding us as substantially different in this respect. One of the saddest things I have heard for a long time was the answer of a mother to the question, 'Do other people react when they see your small baby with two hearing aids?' She said:

> Oh, yes they do . . . I notice it particularly when I get on buses. Before he had the hearing aids people would talk to him and look at him and say he was a nice baby. But often now they just look out of the window, or pretend there isn't a baby there at all, which is very upsetting for me. I still want people to notice him, and make a fuss of him.[1]

Life can be made easier for some disabled people by mechanical and electronic devices, such as sophisticated hearing aids, and telephones which incorporate a teleprinter. More important than all these, though, is the simple need to be accepted, whatever our disabilities.

The problems of those who are both deaf and blind are so enormous as to be almost unimaginable by the majority of people; but again it is basically a matter of developing a workable communication system. It may take a very long time to do that, especially with children born deaf and blind, but at least some progress can almost always be made. Helen Keller was very exceptional in every way, but she remains an example of what can sometimes be achieved. Even if a deaf/blind child only ever succeeds in learning a few basic signs, it can create a bridge to participating in, and understanding, the world.

The National Deaf/Blind Helpers League offers good advice to those encountering such people, but it is actually equally applicable to anyone with a disability:

Those of you who are not disabled, think this over. You do not help us by carrying us about; you do not feed our spirit – the real us – by taking us into your charge. You do it by stimulating us – by standing by when we fumble our way about and make our mistakes, until we learn to do things for ourselves. We have our ego as you have yours. We need to feel that our friends are friends because they accept us as being equal to them in humanity.

One of the most encouraging developments recently has been that of 'self advocacy' by the mentally handicapped. There are now People First groups in many long stay hospitals and Adult Training Centres, which meet to discuss their day-to-day lives, the running of their centres, current affairs, employment, relationships and, perhaps most important of all, issues relating to handicap. There is nothing new in all this really, since people have always got together to discuss issues of relevance and importance to them. What is new is that at last non-handicapped people are listening!

Judith Wood, who has Down's Syndrome, runs a People First group. She says:

> By speaking out you can make yourself better, say what will help, and learn how to ask for what you want. We want more housing, more jobs, and changes in Social Education Centres. We want to justify ourselves and our feelings – like how we don't like the labels we are given.[2]

One of the major achievements of one such group was to remove the word 'ambulance' from the side of the minibus which brought trainees to the centre. Ambulances are for sick people, they explained, and the trainees were not sick.

Once people's needs are explained and recognised, much can be done. The role of computers in communication has become obvious to everyone in recent years, and has been exploited to help handicapped people do ordinary things. Keith Harris, for example, who can only control his tongue, uses a tongue-operated computer to drive his electric wheelchair. Amy Golden, aged four, who has cerebral palsy, uses a BBC microcomputer to talk. Until she had the computer her parents had to play an eternal guessing game; she could only signal 'yes' or 'no' so they had to keep asking 'Do you want this? Or this?' With her voice synthesiser she can now communicate properly and be as assertive as any other child. Computers can also help the mentally handicapped to continue learning, and many severely physically handicapped people work as programmers, something they can do on equal terms with the able bodied.

As an exercise in will power, and to demonstrate the importance of communication, imagine for a moment what life would be like if you had, say, cerebral palsy, and were unable to talk at all, or co-ordinate your hand movements sufficiently to spell out words on a board. Before he mastered the intricacies of his typing system, Christopher Nolan could only signal two words – 'Yes', by looking up and 'no', by blinking twice. As part of the exercise, suppose that you want something very simple like a drink of water.

You look hard at a cup until someone notices (which could take varying amounts of time depending on your environment and how observant your companions are). Then the ordeal begins! They ask, 'Do you want tea?' You blink twice. 'Coffee?' Blink twice. Cocoa?' Blink twice. 'Orange Juice?' Blink twice. 'Lemonade?' Blink twice. 'Water?' At last! Look up!

Are you thinking that you would probably just give in and put up with the tea? Yet it should not need to be so.

The concept of Bliss symbols was developed many years ago for people faced with just this kind of frustration. The basic system is a large grid on which are printed words or pictures which the user looks at or points to. This is all very well, but it can be very frustrating indeed unless the 'listener' catches on quickly. Now, a computer and printer can be used to display a standard Bliss symbols board, the user selecting what he wants to say by using an up/down left/right indicator on the screen. This is a lot quicker, and may also have the added advantage of being used to switch on and off radio, TV or lights, or even to synthesise a voice.

All this is really just a question of tapping the resources

hidden within a severely disabled person incapable of communicating by conventional means. The poet C.P. Cavafy explained how it feels to be trapped by such a situation when he said, of being in a foreign country whose language he did not understand, 'I suffered no little discomfort, having whole conversations stacked inside me.' Now, at last, computers are enabling handicapped people to have these conversations.

But what about those whose inability to communicate is more than just physical? Perhaps the hardest people of all to communicate with are those suffering from autism. They simply cannot make sense of language or gesture. They seem almost impossible to communicate with as babies, either never making a sound at all, or screaming virtually all the time. Most show no interest or reaction when spoken to, and though they do try to understand what is being said, eventually they just give up – it is too difficult a task even to contemplate.

Maybe it is not unlike the situation of someone who can speak a couple of sentences of French giving up when they are confronted with a whole room of French speakers. Autistic people do sometimes try to talk, it is true, but often it is only to echo things they have heard other people say – they nearly always have great difficulty understanding any sort of language, verbal or not. Nevertheless some have the most amazing abilities. Stephen Wiltshire is one example. At the age of thirteen he is considered by many to be the best child artist in the country. He can draw buildings accurately down to the last detail, completely from memory and after only looking at them for a couple of minutes. Yet, being autistic, he finds standard methods of communication almost impossible.[3]

Autistic people, who are unable to communicate in conventional ways, may seem beyond the help of anyone but 'experts', but this is not necessarily true. Ann Lovell, in her book *Simple Simon* explains how her autistic son brought her back to Christ.

I take Simon to church and especially when I lead him up to the communion rail and kneel beside him, I have an overwhelming feeling that both he and I are in the right place. For all his vulnerability, he is absolutely safe there, surrounded and borne up by everyone's life. For my part, I am safe in the knowledge that I am understood. And so back in my pew again, I watch the others, the halt, and the blind, and the very old and the very ill, being lovingly and reverently led and supported to and from that table. I feel this is the very heart of Christianity, alive and beating, and that it is not the strong, the speech-makers and the layers-down-of-the-law who are closest to it, but the weak. Who, in fact, it occurs to me to wonder, is leading whom in the walk to the banquet?[4]

Fortunately there are few people who have the same degree of difficulty in communicaton as the autistic. Much more often we come across people who have a stammer, or other speech impediment, and are usually very wary of drawing attention to their problem or making them nervous. Even stammers can have their compensations, though. Aneurin Bevan, who was largely responsible for setting up the National Health Service, had a severe stammer as a child, which he never completely lost. He used to say that the richness of his vocabulary was due to persistently having to search in dictionaries for alternatives to the words he had trouble with.

Art and music have long been recognised as peculiarly human forms of communication, which speak to us on a very deep emotional level. These are things many handicapped people can appreciate and enjoy, even if few excel to the same degree as Stephen Wiltshire.

I began piano lessons at the same time as I was learning to read, and feel much gratitude to my parents that they brought the ability to communicate through music into my life so young. I play several instruments now, and have in the past been in orchestras and bands. I frequently take refuge in music at difficult times, finding that it can console and also teach me things which are beyond words and conscious language.

Blind people can also find enjoyment in music, and braille transcripts of music are easily available. Many non-handicapped people seem to feel that blindness would be the most difficult handicap to overcome, but that doesn't appear to be actually the case. Generally, blind people function much more easily in society than those who are deaf, largely because their powers of communication are not affected. The poet Milton, whose major work, *Paradise Lost*, was written when he was totally blind wrote, 'I have lost only the inconsequential skin of things.'

People who are deaf are sometimes treated as if they are unable to observe anything either, or notice that people are talking about them. Blind people say that it is often assumed by strangers that they are deaf too. Once more, this could probably largely be avoided if there were more contact between handicapped and able bodied people. Something every handicapped person has to steel themselves against, regardless of whether or not they have severe communication problems, is what I will call 'stereotyped conversations', which actually benefit no one at all.

Everyone in a wheelchair knows the totally frustrating experience of being regarded as completely incapable of any normal response. Many is the time I have been almost deafened by being shouted at as if I can't hear, and quite often people pushing my chair have been asked, 'Can she hear me?' On one memorable occasion a schoolfriend I was with was asked, as the speaker pointed a finger at me, 'Can *he* hear me?' which was disconcerting to say the least!

I appeal to those who push people in wheelchairs to help minimise this type of degrading incident. Please don't talk to passers-by with the wheelchair positioned so that it is facing away from the conversation. This means that the occupant has to either twist round uncomfortably, or feel bored and not a little silly sitting staring into space, and in either case is effectively excluded from the conversation. Also, please don't rock a wheelchair back and forth like a pram. We are not babies and don't want to be sent to sleep!

Naturally any initial contact with a new acquaintance can cause self-consciousness, as I know myself, since I am very nervous of other people. This is perhaps more acute than usual when one person is disabled, and the other feels aware of staring, even if actually they are not. Additionally, eye contact is a very important form of body language, and if the disabled person has unco-ordinated movements, or is unable to respond with nods of the head and other positive signals, the conversation can seem awkward and stilted. Even the fact that wheelchair users are so low down can cause minor problems – either the able bodied person has to be uncomfortable crouching down, or the disabled one gets a crick in the neck! Once you know each other, of course, this type of thing is hardly noticed at all.

Some interesting research has shown that in interacting with the disabled, people do tend to feel they must consider carefully each topic of conversation before embarking on it, which again can cause tension initially. Should you, for instance talk to someone in a wheelchair about 'going for a walk'? Or tell the blind of what you saw? Or the deaf of what you heard? The answer is, of course, yes you should. If the conversation is to be natural and unstressed it needs to be as normal as possible. Also, 'I see what you mean' or 'I heard from my sister' don't necessarily imply actual physical sight or hearing; neither does my saying 'I'm going for a walk' necessarily mean getting my crutches out and actually walking. They are just figures of speech; but even when they are not it is no big deal. Hearing about people climbing mountains or running and jumping does not upset me. They are simply things I haven't experienced – as also are, for instance, going to China, or speaking Portuguese.

Some able bodied people get so worried about trivialities like this that they can hardly concentrate on what *is* being said, and may thus come away with no idea at all of what was being discussed. A particularly good example of this occurred when I was speaking to a group in a College of Further Education about the problems of disability. I had just returned from the United States, and as an exercise I asked the students to think about the difficulties I might have had on the plane. One woman's answer was 'The working surfaces would be too high!'

At the other extreme, curiosity or downright revulsion and incomprehension by strangers is something most disabled people dread more than anything else. This is especially true for those with facial deformities, whose handicap is almost solely the reaction of others to their physical appearance. I very rarely look at people when I am out, I suppose because I am afraid of bad reactions. It is bad enough for me, but it can be even worse for those with more severe disabilities. Carol and Gareth Cole, who both have cerebral palsy, discovered how bad it can get when they asked for a bottle of wine at a restaurant, and then heard the waitress ask the manager, 'Can these people have wine?'[5]

Problems seem to arise most often because people are looking only at the disability and not at the person who has it – something that is underlined when people try to help me by lifting my chair out of the car, but don't listen to my instructions. This generally results in pieces of it falling off in their hands, after which I would guess they heartily resolve not to 'help' a handicapped person again.

Then again, there are those who regard anyone with a disability as an eternal child, which happens frequently to those who are very small of stature, and those with a mental handicap. My friend Debby Wakeham, the mother of a mildly mentally handicapped young man, suggests that we should never assume that non-speaking people are incapable of understanding also. She always talked to David, even though he hardly answered at all until he was five. Now, at eighteen, he talks about things which happened when he was two.

Finally, I would like to say something to those people who feel they cannot cope with another person's pain. They wonder how they can reasonably talk to those who have suffered far more than they have themselves, thinking perhaps especially of those who have been disabled as a result of deliberate violent acts – who have been shot, or knifed, or raped and mutilated, or are the victims of a bomb blast. The tragic case of David, a six-year-old boy in America deliberately set on fire by his father, now terribly burned and scarred for life[6] maybe sums up the enormity of these situations. It can be very difficult for those who are healthy in body, mind and spirit to identify and communicate with people like this, with the question always in the back of their mind, 'How would I cope with this awful thing?' or even, 'How can they still be ordinary people like me, after this tragedy?' There are no easy questions, but the following prayer may help a little. It was written in Ravensbruck concentration camp, by an unknown prisoner, and left by the body of a dead child:

> O Lord, remember not only the men and women of good will, but also those of ill will. But do not remember all the suffering they have inflicted on us; remember the fruits we have bought, thanks to this suffering – our comradeship, our loyalty, our humility, our courage, our generosity, the greatness of heart which has grown out of all this; and when they come to judgement let all the fruits which we have borne be their forgiveness.[7]

Love must eventually be the answer to every problem, large or small. It was demonstrated to me in a gentle yet powerful way when I visited Lourdes – the only place in the world where I have ever *not* been stared at, not ignored or talked down to by shopkeepers and passers-by, not made to feel a curiosity. In Lourdes, for five days, I became in the eyes of other people what I am in my own eyes – an ordinary person who happens to have a disability which shows.

The same spirit of love is revealed in this poem by John Wilkins, a mentally handicapped trainee at an Adult Education Centre:

> Put away that gun
> We human beings everyone
> And love is now our heart
> is to love
> for that's
> what we're put on earth to do[8]

Ask yourself

(1) What are the most important things you communicate a) with your family?   b) with others in your community?

(2) *What help can churchgoers give to those with communication problems a) practically?   b) in terms of tolerance and patience?*

(3) *Should finger spelling be taught in schools? How can lipreaders be helped to full communication? (Consider, for example, where you should sit so the most effective light falls on your lips; whether you should shave off a moustache or beard!)*

(4) *Can anything be done to prevent patronising attitudes and stereotyped conversations? If so, what?*

(5) *Is it better to kneel down when talking to someone in a wheelchair, or to tower over them?*

(6) *How can we learn to communicate better with those who have a mental handicap?*

7

Your Worst Fears Realised

So far I have been talking about 'handicapped people' as though we were a fairly homogenous group, but while there are obviously common experiences there are also very big differences according to the type of handicap and what caused it.

I have heard quite often discussions along the lines of 'Is it worse to be born handicapped, or to become handicapped?', the consensus usually resolving that it is better to have a congenital handicap. Then at least, the argument goes, you have never known any different.

So I want now to think about how people with different handicaps are treated, why the cause of the handicap should make a difference to this, and how a more rational attitude about the matter could help towards the acceptance of all disabled people.

Discrimination against the congenitally handicapped is much worse, as is obvious to everyone now. Whereas people with an acquired handicap are looked after and rehabilitated, there is an almost universal enthusiasm for killing the congenitally handicapped before birth. The diagnosis of spina bifida or Down's Syndrome seems a quite sufficient reason to justify abortion in the minds of, according to the polls, 89 per cent of people in this country. Yet those who become similarly handicapped later in life, say by spinal cord injury, or brain damage following car accidents, are not regarded as being 'better off dead'. This is incongruous because generally it is viewed as worse to acquire a handicap – yet they are not the ones who are being killed off.

Fear of handicap is almost instinctive in all of us, and it naturally takes time for most parents to adjust to the possibility of it happening to their children. It's an adjustment that begins, if not before birth, only a few seconds after, when the first question they ask after, 'Is it a boy or a girl?' is 'Is it all right?' There is such a negative attitude to disability generally that being told your baby is not all right can seem like an unmitigated disaster, even though time may well prove that this is far from the truth.

A very extreme case might provide a good starting-place for thinking about handicap in a rational, dispassionate way. In the past year or so there have been reports in the newspapers of babies born with two heads.[1] The reaction of most people not connected with pro-life or Christian groups seems to have been that these 'monsters' ought to be swiftly killed; or failing that, that one head ought to be severed, so that some semblance of 'normality' is restored. Some tabloid newspapers have gone so far as to label these unfortunate babies 'aliens' or 'sons of Satan', and the thought of allowing them to continue living as they are seems impossible to many people. Yet is it to benefit the babies, or themselves, that they feel alarmed enough to suggest this extreme course of action?

Conjoined twins have always been regarded as fascinating, ever since Chang and Eng Bunker (the original 'Siamese' twins) were brought to public attention. They were never separated, and were exhibited in Barnum and Bailey's Circus before getting married to two sisters and having numerous children. More recently the story of Yvonne and Yvette Jones, American sisters joined at the head, has hit the headlines. They are now attending college and regard themselves not as deformed or handicapped, but just as 'different', perhaps because their mother always taught them to think of themselves as individuals who were special. They were the work of God, she explained, and this was something to be accepted, not rejected. The twins themselves have no problems with their condition, but when they go out crowds part, traffic screeches to a halt, and some people cover their eyes in disgust.[2]

Yet again, the problem is really with the able bodied, who are simply scared of the unknown. But if Yvonne and Yvette can live ordinary lives (providing they are allowed by society to do so), why not also the two-headed babies? There is nothing inherently 'wrong' with having two heads, or being

71

joined to someone else. What is wrong is the mentality that says such people should be eliminated.

Perhaps the main difficulty is that able bodied people find it hard to view any kind of physical or mental 'difference' as normal; though of course to me and my family and friends it is quite ordinary for me to be this shape. My disability has undoubtedly caused some traumas – for my family, coping with my illnesses and operations, for me, being in hospital a lot, suffering pain, learning to live with curiosity and discrimination. However, the hardest parts of my life, including my divorce, have had nothing to do with disability, but everything to do with the emotional responses and relationships of an average human being.

That people find this hard to understand is demonstrated time and again, particularly in this country, by the assumption that having spina bifida must mean that I have a particular type of personality to go with it. Interestingly enough, in the USA I have generally found that people regard my being from England as far more interesting than the fact of my disability. Here, however, there seems often to be a desperate desire to classify and label me as either a) someone who was once 'normal', b) someone who is only temporarily in the ranks of the 'abnormal' or c) someone who has always, irrevocably, been 'abnormal'. This is a very serious matter, but it does have its funny side – like when I have been asked, 'Were you born in a wheelchair?' One day, I know, I will yield to the almost irresistible impulse to reply, 'Yes, my mother had a very difficult delivery!'

The people who suffer most from this type of labelling are probably the mentally handicapped, because the advances in the treatment of conditions like Down's Syndrome are not yet common knowledge, and because it is much more difficult to imagine having a mental handicap than it is to visualise being limited in a purely physical way. The game I propose you try in order to get an idea what mental handicap feels like is a little complicated, but it is good fun, and could almost be done as a kind of party game:

(1) Place a cardboard box on its base, open side up, on a table.

(2) Cut a hole just big enough for your hand to go through, in one side of the box, and then put some paper in the bottom of it.

(3) Put your hand, holding a pen, through the hole into the box.

(4) Hold or position a mirror (or get someone to hold one for you) so you can see the reflection of your hand, the pen and the paper. You must not be able to see them directly.

(5) Try to copy shapes, or letters, or draw pictures, or write your name, using only the reflected image in the mirror.

See what I mean? No matter how hard you try, or how hard you concentrate, you make a mess of it time and again; which may give just an inkling of how mental handicap actually feels. One interesting observation is that if you get others to try this game too, you will discover that no two people find it difficult in exactly the same way, which is relevant to those who actually have a handicap – no two of them are the same.

Rex Brinkworth was the first person in this country to introduce a method of treatment and training for children with Down's Syndrome. He was awarded the MBE for his work with these children over twenty-seven years, and he maintains that they are no more alike than any other group of people who have had somewhat similar life experiences. His system has demonstrated many times just how much people with a mental handicap can achieve, by a combination of dietary supplements, education and training. Remembering the doctor's words when his daughter Françoise was born – 'What a pity, she will never be more than a vegetable' – he takes great delight in pointing out that at the age of twenty-two she can now read, play the piano, type, operate a word processor and drive a car. When she accompanied him to Buckingham Palace to collect his MBE she remarked that without her he would never have got it. True enough, as his methods, now used all over the world, were first developed to help Françoise. Rex says that 'As long as a child has a brain at all, it has a computer more complex than

73

any man can make'; which is rather a sobering thought for those who believe the mentally handicapped are not worth bothering with.

I feel angry when I think of the 'hopeless' prognosis given to so many new parents of handicapped children. If doctors really have 'no hope', I think they should at least wait to see what happens, because the vast majority of handicapped people are quite as full of hopes and dreams as the able bodied. I will not deny that there have been times, when I have felt without hope, but then so have very many people. If some handicapped people are miserable, and others with the same limitations are happy and fulfilled, it must surely be something other than the handicap which is causing the unhappiness. In which case, there is no reason to say that handicap 'causes misery'.

At the time of the thalidomide tragedy, the children born damaged by the drug were regarded as being completely without hope, to such an extent that the whole affair speeded up the passing of the Abortion Act. Later, Madeleine Simms and Keith Hindell of the Abortion Law Reform Association dedicated a book to the mothers of thalidomide children 'for whom reform came too late', the obvious implication being that they would have been better off dead.

One person who would not agree is Louise Medus, born without arms or legs as a result of her mother taking thalidomide. She is now a wife and mother herself, she and her husband having decided before the baby's birth that they would love it 'no matter what, disabled or not.' Louise explained, 'My philosophy is, where there's a will there's a way. Whether you want to get a job, marry or have a child, you can always find a way. There are no excuses.'

Instances of people with congenital handicaps, who might well now be aborted but who hold similar views to Louise, are more commonplace than rare. A few examples will show what I mean:

My friend Marilyn Carr was born without arms (not a thalidomide-induced handicap, but just one of those things). She is married, drives a car, and has written an autobiography called *Look, No Hands*. She stood for Parliament in

1981 as an Independent Pro-life candidate.

Jeffrey Tate, principal conductor of the Royal Opera, conducts sitting down, 'except in moments of extreme emotion'. He has spina bifida.

Nabil Shaban is an actor who has appeared on television many times, acting different roles and also defending the right to life of the handicapped. He is less than three feet tall and confined to a wheelchair because he was born with brittle bones.

Terry Dicks is a conservative MP who says, 'Every child has the right to life, no matter what disability it may be born with.' He has cerebral palsy.

Ellen Wilkie is a poet, writer, actress, classics graduate and presenter of the Channel 4 programme 'Same Difference'. She has muscular dystrophy and says, 'I lead a perfectly normal life, with a fulfilling, enjoyable career.'

Alison John has cerebral palsy, is married to a curate, and appeared with Terry Wogan on television. Polly Toynbee, reporting the meeting in the *Guardian* said, 'People ought to see in her a very remarkable woman, a delightful character and a fierce intelligence.'[3] Yes indeed; but what is incongruous is that Polly Toynbee also thinks that 'If the new test which detects abnormality at a much earlier stage passes its experimental phase, it must be made universally available as soon as possible.'[4] This is exactly the same mentality as that held by the Nazis, and ought to be recognised as such. Meanwhile, it is hard for me not to reach the conclusion that the world would be a much safer and pleasant place for me and those like me if there were more Alison Johns in it, not fewer.

The situation of those with very severe handicaps, who will inevitably live short lives, is slightly different, but they are still entitled to respect as individuals, and to a natural death when their time comes. There could be no more severe handicap than anencephaly – the absence of most of the brain. Such babies are considered as dispensable now that some doctors are using them as organ donor banks while they are still alive.[5]

Paul Johnson eloquently describes what this means to him.

As the father of an anencephalic boy, I know he could feel pain. He developed a clear personality, showing pleasure by smiling, displeasure by become agitated; he could even follow you round the room with his eyes. The only time he cried was when he was dying – a really pitiful heart-rending sound, which clearly showed his pain and distress. I feel sick at the thought of babies like my son dying under the surgeon's scalpel.[6]

Perhaps the best person to epitomise the value of life for the severely congenitally handicapped, was Jethro Carpenter. He was unable to walk, talk, feed or control his head. He needed oxygen and suction equipment available twenty-four hours a day, as his parents never knew when he might need to be resuscitated. He would always have been doubly incontinent. In spite of all this, he really did live his life to the full. He smiled and laughed, like any other child; he even threw the odd temper tantrum. Before his death at the age of two, his mother, Jill, said:

If anyone does not agree he has a right to life, come to my home and spend time here, and tell me where it is that either we or Jethro are handicapped in the sense of not having a full life. Where is it that we are so deprived? Most of all tell me what we would have got out of having an abortion. All I can show is what we would have lost.

James Watson, Nobel Prize winner and joint discover with Francis Crick of the double helix of human DNA, thought that babies should only be declared human after three days, so that they could first be checked for handicap, and only the 'normal' would be allowed membership of the human family.[7] Jesus Christ, on the other hand, said of a man born blind that neither he nor his father had sinned, but that his blindness existed in order that the works of God might be made manifest. I think the case of Jethro Carpenter shows quite clearly which of these is right.

The thought of suddenly becoming disabled is an alarming prospect for most able bodied people, not just because of the physical and emotional adjustments that would have to be made, but also because anyone who has even suffered a broken leg knows how disabled people are treated.

Perhaps the most important thing to remember, for example after spinal cord injury, is that the person is still the same individual, even though they may at first be depressed, frustrated, angry or simply wondering how on earth they are going to cope. There are great physical adjustments to be made, of course, but also the attitudes and responses of the rest of society play a part in shaping their altered outlook.

Mary Greaves explains the devastating change in attitude which sometimes happens.

> I was just an ordinary little girl, with fair curly hair, wearing dresses made by my mother. Until suddenly one day in November when I was three-and-a-half years old, I ceased being a little girl and became 'a polio'.[8]

It is easy to see what an effect this could have on a person already suffering the problems of a new disability – it is also easy to see how unnecessary it is.

In fact there are generally much better services, rehabilitation and benefits for those whose disability is acquired, especially if it can be blamed on an individual or a company; and as I have already shown, they often find it easier to be accepted into society than those born handicapped.

The adjustments newly disabled people have to make would of course be a lot more straightforward if examples of disability in literature and the media were more honest. However, I have pointed out, disabled people are generally portrayed as courageous angels, pitiful victims, or alternatively as 'hopeless', unless there is some prospect of them getting better – almost everyone can remember from their childhood the story of Heidi and her crippled friend Clara who, it seems, only needs to get a whiff of clean Swiss mountain air to get her up on her feet. Unfortunately (or fortunately, perhaps!) real life isn't quite like that.

There is a stigma attached to all disability, as well as a major assault on the self concept of a previously able bodied person. In fact, it seems as if a kind of bereavement often has to be gone through, before acceptance and resumption of normal life can take over. This is obviously particularly difficult with degenerating conditions like multiple sclerosis; people with this disease can be walking one day and in a wheelchair the next; or fine for years and then suddenly overwhelmed by tiredness, weakness, double vision and incontinence; and the uncertainty is terribly difficult to come to terms with. Mary Corrigan, who has MS asked me to say, in the context of other people's attitude to her illness, that she would like to ask them only to enquire how she is if they really want to know, and are prepared for a negative or complicated answer. This seems like sound advice anyway, since it hardly seems worth bothering to ask, if any answer but 'fine' will be unacceptable.

The problems faced by people with terminal illnesses are different in some ways, but the same general rule still holds true – they are ordinary individuals who now have special needs. Everyone is now becoming aware of people dying of AIDS, who need to be regarded as dignified human beings, suffering a tragic illness, not undergoing a just punishment.

What is perhaps not so well known is the plight of those with degenerative diseases like Huntington's Chorea. This is a hereditary condition which leads to physical and mental deterioration – at first unsteadiness, forgetfulness and irritability, which leads on to inability to walk, talk or swallow properly, and then finally to death.

There is a 50 per cent chance of passing Huntington's Chorea on to the children of affected people, but by the time they realise they have the disease, they may already have had children. Now there is a predictive test available, so people at risk can find out if they have the relevant gene, but it is a terribly difficult decision to have to make. Is it better to know you will probably suffer and die in a particularly distressing way, or just to wait and see if it happens?

One would think that this must be the worst misfortune anyone could experience, yet even so, life can still be precious. I wrote an article for the Association of Huntington's Chorea when it first became apparent that a pre-natal screening test would soon be available to detect the gene in time for abortion. Among the many replies I received, both hostile and supportive, was one from Mary Whyte, who said,

> My family is being totally decimated by Huntington's Chorea – my husband dead, my eldest daughter and her two sons now also stricken, as well as a sister-in-law. The suffering is great, but all life is wonderful.

She advised me to 'Stick to it – there aren't many of us around.' People like Mary have much to teach everyone, including me, about life and its real meaning.

It seems that, whatever the disability and however severe it is, there will be at least *someone* who thinks life is nevertheless very much worth living. Ann Armstrong, who has been totally paralysed and in an iron lung for thirty years following an attack of polio says, 'Physically I am rather a useless creature. But I still have no regrets. I'm still able in spirit to do so much for my family and friends.'[9] People with different types of illness and disability, even the terminally ill, can still enjoy life and be happy. Gaervan Byrne, who had leukaemia and died at the age of twelve, knew he hadn't long to live when I last met him, yet he spoke quite happily of how he would watch over his family once he had gone to be with God. He just knew there was no need to be afraid or worried, and he relied on the greatest assurance of all that everything would indeed turn out well.

Strangely enough, sometimes those with only marginal disabilities seem to suffer more problems. This is borne out by studies which show that in general, for instance, completely blind people are better adjusted than the partially sighted, and totally deaf people better than the partially hearing.

I can remember very well children at school who wore glasses and were ridiculed far more than me for their very minimal handicap. Children of mixed race, and those who are very fat, who are really not 'handicapped' at all, can suffer tremendously from the cruelty of other people, the memory of which stays with them forever.

It is conditions like partial deafness, epilepsy, and incontinence unconnected to other disabilities, which seem to cause most problems, and some people with these conditions go to great lengths to avoid situations in which they might be 'found out'. They may even withdraw completely because they cannot tolerate the anxiety of never knowing if and when an awkward situation might arise.

To a lesser extent, this happens at times to able bodied people. If you are the only Christian at your school or place of work, you might be laughed at or made to feel the odd one out, which is hard for anyone, even the most self confident, to cope with. However, an added problem for people with handicap is generally that the person is also 'marginalised' in their own family, which means they are only really 'normal' with other disabled people. Knowing only too well how disability is regarded by society in general, many people with a marginal handicap desperately want to avoid being labelled 'handicapped' and try very hard to pass instead as being able bodied. This can lead to a lot of problems.

Here is another game for you to try:

Imagine, for a moment, that you are an epileptic. You work in an office as a typist, and enjoy the work very much. No one there knows you are subject to occasional fits, because they generally happen in the evenings, and are in any case controlled most of the time by anti-convulsant drugs. When you do have a fit, however, it can be alarming for the uninitiated.

One day you are invited by your boss to go out for a drink in the evening. You didn't tell him about your condition at the time of the interview, and are only too well aware that even now some people view epilepsy as a form of insanity. Do you:

(a) Make some excuse for not going, which may make you appear unsociable, and may lose you friends?
(b) Go, but make an excuse to leave after half an hour?
(c) Weigh up how likely it is that you will have a fit that particular evening (the kind of delicate equation which has very serious consequences if you get it wrong)?

(d) Go, and hope for the best, remembering that if the worst happens you could well lose your job?

(e) Tell someone you work with what may happen and what to do if it does?

Whatever you decided to do, it is obvious that the whole exercise would cause a lot of stress. And even if everything went well, how would you have reacted if people started telling jokes about epilepsy? The same kind of dilemma confronts partially hearing people, who have to decide whether to pretend to be absent minded to cover up for missing parts of a conversation, or to reveal their condition and risk alienation or incomprehension.

These are very difficult decisions for the people affected, but everything would be made so much easier if disability was regarded as ordinary – a thing that happens to some people, is perhaps regrettable, but may in fact be a positive force for good, if it is viewed in the right way.

My answer to the question, 'Is it better to be born handicapped or become handicapped?' is that neither is 'better' or 'worse', but both offer a unique opportunity to develop and grow in different ways. However, I will leave the last word in this chapter to Elisabeth Buggins, because she sums it all up so well. Elisabeth had three haemophiliac sons, one of whom was also mentally handicapped and died a few years ago. She told me:

> It may seem strange but I love what has happened to me. This handicap of haemophilia is my greatest treasure because it has changed my understanding of and objectives in life, and enriched my closest relationships far beyond the potential of wealth or success. The family have been together through the fires and know that our love and kinship is a bedrock which remains when all the façades are burnt away and social norms meaningless. That, and a loving God who is totally just, trustworthy and kind, is strength. I can't give new parents coping with this problem faith, or professional advice or magic solutions. What I can give them is understanding, and encouragement to listen to the feelings within themselves,

and to know that grief, even the greatest, can be – not got over, but lived into and incorporated into one's living, so that life is enriched.

Ask yourself

(1) What kind of handicap do you think would be 'worst'? Why?

(2) Why do you think society has different attitudes to those with a congenital handicap and those who acquire a handicap?

(3) What can able bodied people do to help remove the stress suffered by those with a marginal handicap?

(4) How would you cope with a degenerating illness, such as multiple sclerosis?

8

The Slippery Slope

'It seems to me as clear as daylight that abortion would be a crime,' wrote Mahatma Gandhi in *All Men are Brothers*.

One of the most difficult decisions facing parents today in countries where there is legalised abortion is what they will do if they discover their unborn child is handicapped. Even by saying that I have already made a subtle statement about what is currently accepted as the most sensible and humane decision – because I said, 'If they discover' the handicap. And of course the only way they can discover it is by taking advantage of the general enthusiasm for pre-natal screening programmes, whose object is to detect and abort the handicapped.

Once handicap has been detected, abortion is not only seen as acceptable, but is often positively encouraged. And wherever abortion is promoted as the proper solution to the problems of disability, those who have already been born with similar handicaps find their own rights on increasingly shaky ground. For if it is decided that it is both right and proper to kill someone because they have a particular condition, why should others with that same condition be accorded rights simply because they are older? Nevertheless, societies all over the world are deciding that it is desirable to eliminate the handicapped at the earliest possible moment.

Societies have always existed to promote and protect the rights and freedoms of their members, and opposition to deliberate killing by abortion has an equally long history. The Hippocratic Oath, written 400 years B C, prohibited doctors from performing abortions; and in the third century A D the Roman historian and theologian Tertullian condemned it as a form of homicide.

However, alongside this firmly held belief in the rights of all human beings, including the unborn, there often seems to have been the unspoken exception of those born handicapped. This has manifested itself through the ages, from the exposing of deformed infants in ancient Sparta, to the hushed-up so-called 'stillbirths' of Victorian England, to the attitude currently held that the unborn have no rights unless they are 'wanted', and that handicap is 'prevented' if the handicapped are prevented from living.

Since it is almost impossible to argue that the unborn are not human and alive, many people try to say that they don't yet have the status of 'persons', and so have fewer rights. One prominent pro-abortionist once went so far as to say in a debate that she also considered *me* to be a 'non person' and that if I were to be killed it would not really be murder. I wonder if that status would make me immune from the law if I killed her? Maybe she should just be glad that I am pro life!

While all this argument is going on, some doctors are using the uncertainty to persuade new and vulnerable parents that their handicapped baby's life would inevitably be short and miserable (hardly a life at all, in fact), and should therefore be snuffed out quickly. One 'eminent paediatrician' stated in the *British Medical Journal* that what he had to offer spina bifida babies with my degree of handicap was 'some help in hastening the end of a life which I have to advise the parents would otherwise be one which is not a life in any full sense.'[1] If that is 'eminence', I think I will make a point of asking to see a retarded doctor next time I am ill.

Quality of life is sometimes regarded as the crucial factor in deciding if a baby should live; but the problem is, how can we judge quality? And why should it only be considered if the baby is handicapped? Not all able bodied people have a quality of life which is good by conventional standards, but we don't try to predict at birth, or even before, if *their* lives will be 'worth living'. Imagine the parents of a normal baby being asked to decide before its birth whether it will be happy and productive, in which case it may be born, or miserable and unproductive (maybe mentally ill, or depressed, or unemployed, or a drug addict) in which case it should be aborted *for its own good*.

Handicapped people are just as much individuals as the

able bodied and the quality of their lives covers roughly the same spectrum. Severity of handicap is not a useful factor in deciding how happy an individual has the capacity to be – unless, that is, you accept the concept that people who wear glasses are slightly less happy than those who don't, or that Olympic athletes are supremely happy and people like me inevitably suicidal.

I do of course realise that some parents could not cope with a handicapped child; though I think many more could, given appropriate care and support from the community. Adoption is the obvious non-violent solution to problems like this, and contrary to popular belief, even severely handicapped children can and do get adopted.

Ten years ago or so, it was quite unusual for this to happen, but now, according to Philip Stogdon, a social worker with Parents for Children, for every 'unwanted' Down's Syndrome baby 'we have ten families to choose from, and we can also find placements for children with cerebral palsy, or epilepsy, for spastic quadriplegics or blind children'.[2] Children with spina bifida are also, apparently, easy to place with adoptive families.

The British Association for Adoption and Fostering, through its 'Be my Parent' catalogues and videos, has placed many handicapped children, sometimes with people previously considered 'unsuitable' to adopt. These include the unemployed and single parents – Lucy Baxter, for instance, a single mother who has adopted two Down's Syndrome boys and freely admits, 'I honestly can't visualise life without them'.[3] Also, it is becoming increasingly recognised that disabled people should also be allowed to adopt, and deaf people are now often considered as ideal adoptive parents for deaf children.

In fact age, rather than handicap, is often seen by adoption agencies as the main difficulty in placing children, but this is by no means always the case. I first met Helen Ross at an SPUC conference four years ago. She was then a teenager, mentally and physically handicapped, confined to a wheelchair, unable to speak, and blind. She was there with her mother Eileen, and I was delighted to meet them both. Shortly after that Eileen died, and I was quite worried about what would happen to Helen. Imagine my happiness, then, when at last year's conference, I saw Helen with her adopted mother, Colleen Lowden. Both Helen and Colleen were fit and well, and the relationship had obviously been of great benefit to them both.

Although pro-life people are frequently accused of not understanding the problems of disability, and never adopting handicapped children themselves, my experience has proved exactly the opposite. Many members of the SPUC Handicap Division have adopted handicapped children, the latest being the Payne family. Harry and Julie Payne and their sons Andrew, Robert and Martin fostered Rebecca, who has Down's Syndrome and a serious heart condition, when she was only seven months old. Now aged three, she has just become their adopted daughter. Julie wrote to me to tell me about this happy event:

> I think about her birth-parents and the undoubted sadness that Rebecca's birth brought to them. But I hope the knowledge that she is loved and happy in her adopted family eases their pain, and that they can think of her with love.

Since its inception in 1967 the Abortion Act has killed over three million children, only a small percentage of them handicapped. However these 'eugenic' abortions have been the most publicly acceptable of them all, largely I think because of very basic misconceptions about disability. In parliamentary debates, for instance, Down's Syndrome is usually viewed by pro-abortionists as virtually a fate worse than death, yet none of the many Down's people I know would agree. On the contrary many are genuiely alarmed about abortion and the killing of the newborn handicapped. After the much-publicised death of Down's baby John Pearson at the hands of his doctor, Françoise Brinkworth expressed her disquiet about going into hospital for minor routine surgery, admitting, 'I'm afraid they might do me in.'

Nor is it only people with Down's Syndrome who are so misrepresented. Peter Thurnham MP said in the debate on the second reading of David Alton's Abortion Bill,

> Spina bifida is one of the most serious disabilities that can be detected. Why should mothers be forced to carry a child with spina bifida, when 70 per cent of them die in agony before the age of five, and have to be sedated because of their pain?[4]

The fact that this is quite untrue, and actually a gross distortion of reality seemed not to bother him at all.

Erich Fromm wrote, in *The Art of Loving*, 'When the laws of a country contradict the laws of humanity, the true citizen should choose the laws of humanity' – something I feel is particularly true with regard to our abortion laws.

Perhaps it would be helpful here to consider what abortion has actually led to in Britain in the light of the 'benefits' it was supposed to bring. Some thought every child would be a wanted child; but in fact the rates of child abuse have gone up (and Japan, which has free abortion on demand, has the highest rate of child abuse in the world). Some thought it would liberate women, but in fact it made them open to manipulation and oppression by those with power over them: husbands, boyfriends or doctors. Some felt it would save handicapped children a life of misery, but in fact the rejection and discrimination disabled people suffer has only been compounded by fatal pre- and post-natal prejudice. Abortion is not only wrong in itself; it is wrong because of what it leads to.

It is wrong intrinsically because it kills a human being. Every society thinks killing is wrong when it is done to older people; and no one has yet satisfactorily explained why the general rule should be relaxed just because the victim is young and vulnerable. On the contrary, our whole legal system was designed to protect the weakest and most vulnerable, which the unborn surely are.

The Abortion Act has had consequences for the disabled far beyond what anybody could have envisaged in 1967. It has led not only to the destruction of thousands of handicapped unborn children, but also to the sedation and starvation to death of those who failed to be detected in time for abortion. This has inexorably been extended to calls for euthanasia, both voluntary and for those who are incapable of dissention.

It has led to mentally handicapped women being sterilised[5] and given abortions without their consent, because they are considered to be unsuitable to have children; and it has also caused what are termed 'selective feticide' operations, where the heart of one baby in a multiple pregnancy is pierced so that it bleeds to death, while the others (always the non-handicapped) are allowed to continue living.[6] It has allowed the possibility that in the future 'wrongful life' suits may be considered where adults sue doctors on behalf of children they claim should never have been allowed to be born.[7] And it has meant that experimentation on human embryos can be justified by saying that they might help 'prevent handicap'.[8]

The issue of embryo experimentation is quite a new one, but it will certainly become of crucial importance in the immediate future. We therefore need to be sure how far we are prepared to let scientists go in order to prevent or cure disability.

One might have thought, with the birth of the first 'test-tube' baby, Louise Brown, whose conception in 1978 had been visible to all in the laboratory, that the question 'When does life begin?' would have been answered once and for all. But it is quite amazing how people manage to blind themselves to such obvious facts when they have a vested interest in doing so. In view of this I think it is important to stress that, however useful it might be to pretend otherwise, each human being – whose existence began at conception, who has never existed before, nor will again, and who deserves respect and love from us all – is not of relative value, but of infinite value.

Far from embryo experimentation 'preventing handicap' and doing away with the 'need' for eugenic abortion, it simply creates yet another group of humans deemed dispensible. Abortion, and other ways of eliminating the handicapped, will never stop until people with disabilities are acknowledged as having equal rights, and until we reverse the trend which, in the words of Professor Sir William Liley, is toward deciding 'not that this baby has a disease, but that this baby *is* a disease'.[9] Of course, I am not saying that research into preventing the occurrence of handicap should not go on. But unless it is done with due respect for all the individuals involved, we can only be suspicious of the true motives.

There is some evidence, now, that implanting embryonic neural tissue could regenerate damaged spinal cords, and this could eventually reverse the effects of spinal cord injury, or even of spina bifida. Already foetal brain cells have been implanted into the brains of people suffering from Alzheimer's Disease (senile dementia) and Parkinson's Disease, which is characterised by shaky movements and increasing physical and mental deterioration. The cells have to be taken from very young unborn children, up to about eleven weeks in order to be effective; and there is some evidence that they can actually reverse the effects of these diseases.[10]

I would be being less than honest if I said I had no interest at all in the possibility of a 'cure', but it *is* quite true to say that I would definitely not want it at the expense of ex- perimenting upon or killing my fellow human beings, however young. On a more macabre level, procedures such as this raise the alarming and incongruous spectre of the very real possibility of spina bifida unborn children being used to 'cure' spinal cord injured adults – an 'upside-down' ethic if ever there was one!

People who defend abortion and experimentation always talk about the desire for 'perfect' children as if such persons exist, but they never stop to think about the implications of condemning some characteristics as universally bad. Would Beethoven or Helen Keller have been the incredible people they were, and contributed so much to our world, if they had not been handicapped? Would I be writing this now if I had not been born with spina bifida? (Of course if you are not enjoying this book, you may heartily wish I was not now writing it, but that's principles for you!) It is better not to be disabled, yes. But disability is not the worst thing that can happen to people – certainly no worse than the fate some able bodied people suffer, of starvation, or hopelessness or despair.

As a game, consider the following questions:

(1) Are you now a human being?
(2) Were you also a human being yesterday?
(3) One year ago?
(4) Five years ago?
(5) When did you start being a human person?

I believe I was still the person I call 'me' at all those stages of my life, and also when I was unborn, the secret of my disability, which helped make me what I am today, safe from the prying technology that now kills babies solely because they have the potential to be like me. And I was still me when I was an embryo, when the sperm and egg whose genes had only just met first combined to make me what I am now – a unique person. If you agree, please don't keep it to yourself! Share the good news that all human beings have equal rights from the beginning of their lives to the end. And tell people when you, and I, and they, and everyone else since the beginning of time, began to be 'a person'.

Abortion and embryo experimentation seem to have resulted in the view that it is legitimate to fight for our own rights at the expense of suppressing someone else's very right to exist. This is surely completely incompatible with Christian belief.

Despite all the protestations of mercy, it is clear that a factor uppermost in the minds of many pro-abortionists is simply economics – they don't want the financial burden of handicapped people. This is really no different from the Nazis, who considered the handicapped to be 'economic lumber' who ought to be swiftly dispatched. There exist whole volumes of cost benefit studies on the desirability of killing the handicapped, something Peter Thurnham MP explained to Parliament by saying that 'The financial burden of caring for a severely handicapped child is about £500,000. If one takes into account the cost to the state, that could well be another £500,000.'[11] If it can become too expensive for society to care for people who are ill or in need, how safe is anyone? Even from the most selfish of motives it makes sense to realise how this kind of thinking affects us all.

To have an artificially rosy view of born handicapped people as 'brave, wonderful, courageous people' which, depressingly, so many able bodied people do, is to ignore what is being advocated for the unborn with disabilities. And to say that 'opportunities for the disabled in society have never been better' which our government has a habit of doing, is to treat a moral axiom as if it were a fact. You simply cannot treat with proper respect a group of people you are at the same time going to enormous lengths to eliminate.

I have not always been pro-life myself, so perhaps it would help if I explained briefly what led me to change my mind. When I was a student at university I considered myself, as I still largely do, as a feminist, and regarded 'free abortion on demand' as an essential part of the women's rights 'package'. Basically I did so because I did not want to be burdened with unwanted children. I didn't actually know what an abortion entailed, nor did I want to know. I only knew that I dreaded being unwillingly pregnant more than anything else.

And then . . . I read in the *Guardian* an article that was to change my whole life. It told the story of a couple who had decided to 'allow' their spina bifida baby to die. I read it with a kind of morbid interest, and was angry and upset to know that she had been sedated so she was too sleepy to cry for food, and had thus starved to death. Her doctor had advised the parents to allow this to happen because she could have 'compared herself unfavourably with her able bodied sisters'. She would in fact have been exactly as disabled as I am myself.

I filed the article away and tried desperately to forget it. It was another two years before, having read yet another article condoning the killing of the newborn handicapped, I finally did something. I was splutteringly angry and decided to write to the *Guardian* to get the whole thing out of my system. How very naive I was!

My letter was printed, and almost straight away I started getting letters from pro-life groups. I am sure the only thing that saved these anti-abortion letters from an immediate fiery grave was my rather stubborn nature, which dictated that I actually read every letter I received. I was somewhat surprised by what I discovered.

These groups, whose views I had always despised, were trying to tell me that this killing of the newborn and abortion were linked to and symptomatic of the same ideas; that feminists had been conned by the 'right to choose' slogan, and that people with disabilities could not possibly achieve equality in society until they had first secured their equal right to life. It was impossible to disprove what they were saying, no matter how I tried.

I started to get very uncomfortable with my modified view that abortion on the grounds of handicap was wrong (because it was discriminatory) but that abortion in general was acceptable (because it was 'a woman's right to choose'). I suppose I was simply trying to preserve my own peace of mind so that I could have an abortion without a guilty conscience if I got pregnant myself; but it was a completely illogical view, which needed to be worked through.

So anxious was I that disabled people (i.e. me) should be accorded equal rights, I was advocating that we should have more rights than anyone else. That the unborn handicapped should be protected from abortion, but not the unborn able bodied. A kind of reverse discrimination, if you like, that would not stand up to the slightest examination. The reason for it was plain enough, though, because my motive for holding it was not one of mercy for the unborn, but rather of protecting my right to have an abortion. In retrospect, I think this same feeling underlies the attitude of many people. It is not so much that they deny the humanity of the unborn; but because it will so profoundly affect them if they do acknowledge it, they choose to ignore it.

For myself, the reluctant conclusion that life begins at conception meant I had to change my whole way of thinking, and recognise that it is meaningless to claim for ourselves 'rights' that we would simultaneously deny to others, simply because they are less powerful than we are. The same process might be necessary for people who are new to the issue of handicap, and would rather carry on in blissful ignorance. You can't escape that easily now, because I have shown you that we are ordinary people who need equal treatment. Even though it may involve you in uncomfortable or maybe unpleasant tasks or confrontations, you just cannot say any longer, after reading this book, that you don't know anything about disability.

We should remember the words of Martin Luther King: 'The day has passed for bland euphemism. He who lives with untruth lives in spiritual slavery. Freedom is still the bonus we receive for knowing the truth.'[12]

Ask yourself

(1) Do you think abortion on the grounds of handicap is ever justified because of: a) burden to the parents? b) burden to the state? c) the possibility of a 'miserable life' for the child?

(2) Is adoption an adequate solution for parents who genuinely cannot cope with a handicapped child?

(3) Could abortion on the grounds of handicap ever be done without affecting the status of born handicapped people?

(4) What would you do if you discovered that your unborn child was handicapped (say by Down's Syndrome or spina bifida)?

(5) How can handicapped people speak out most effectively in defence of their right to life?

(6) What can able bodied people do to support our struggle for equal rights before birth as well as after?

(7) When did you last write to a newspaper about the urgent need to protect the right to life of the unborn? (If more than a month ago, please think seriously about doing so!)

9

Over my Dead Body!

In recent years, along with the increase in enthusiasm for aborting the handicapped, there has also been a distinct trend towards an acceptance of killing older handicapped people, under the guise of 'mercy'. Several cases have been brought to court, and in all of them, a lot more sympathy has been shown for the killer than the victim.

In its literal definition of 'a gentle and easy death', euthanasia is something everyone would want when their time comes. Or maybe perhaps I should say 'almost everyone'. I suppose I must be flexible to take into account those perverse John Wayne types who might prefer to 'die with their boots on'.

The trouble with this is that it so easily drifts into an acceptance of letting others decide when this gentle and easy death should happen. It is also very easy for ulterior motives to be obscured by protests that it was, after all, merciful.

In all the cases when handicapped people – babies, children and adults – have been subjected to 'mercy killing', the killers have escaped proper punishment. Perhaps the most famous of these was Dr Leonard Arthur, who in 1981 was accused of murdering John Pearson, a Down's Syndrome baby. The baby had been rejected by his parents, so Dr Arthur put on his cot a notice saying, 'Parents do not want it to survive – Nursing Care Only'. He was then given enough sedative to kill an adult and given no milk at all until he died three days later. During his trial, Dr Arthur was described by the judge as a 'caring and compassionate man', while people with Down's Syndrome were called 'walking time bombs of infection and disease'. Dr Arthur was acquitted.[1]

It has become quite common now for babies with Down's Syndrome who also have a life threatening condition, like blocked intestines, to be denied the simple operation they need. Having once had emergency surgery for blocked intestines myself, I can verify that these babies would be in considerable pain until they finally drifted into unconsciousness. No able bodied child would be left to suffer and die like this. I can't see any good reason why things should be different for those with a handicap.

This state of hopelessness about the handicapped fails totally to take account of the current situation. Rex Brinkworth's system, and the achievements of so many people with Down's Syndrome, prove that true progress can happen – so long as a positive viewpoint is preserved.

Throughout history, congenitally deformed children have been feared and considered 'evil'. The Greeks and Romans killed them, and in Rome parents could kill children up to three weeks old, if they could persuade five neighbours to certify that they were 'monsters'. Things are not so very different now.

The Anglican Church of Canada's Interim Report on Human Life (1977) stated:

> Our sense and emotion lead us to the grave mistake of treating human looking shapes as if they were human . . . In fact the only way to treat such deformed infants humanely is not to treat them as human.

A book by the Australian philosophers Peter Singer and Helga Kuhse, entitled *Should the Baby Live?* opens by stating 'This book contains conclusions some readers will find disturbing. We think some infants with severe disabilities should be killed.' A MORI Poll conducted in 1981 seemed to concur with this view since it found that 86 per cent of people thought that doctors should not be found guilty of murder if they killed a severely handicapped baby – which possibly explains why many doctors are now so open about it.

Dr Garrow of High Wycombe, for instance, stated on television that a spina bifida baby in his hospital died of 'a combination of dehydration, infection which we weren't treating, and starvation'. He called this 'the loving thing to do', and said he was simply 'letting nature take its course'.[2]

But this is not what the public thought when a couple were sent to prison for deliberately starving their normal baby to death.[3] Didn't they also only 'allow him to die'? Could we refuse to operate on someone with appendicitis and 'let nature take its course?' Should we do the same with the starving in Ethiopia?

Some doctors even try to deny that they are actually killing these babies. Professor Lorber of Sheffield, who has strict criteria for deciding which spina bifida babies should live (almost all of which I fail), maintains that giving only water until a baby dies does *not* constitute starvation. I'd like to bet he would soon change his mind if I did it to him! He also says that those with normal intelligence suffer more than the mentally handicapped, and thus would be better killed.[4]

Professor Lorber admits that 'there are some babies we do not operate on because we want them to die.'[5] Perhaps doctors with his views should bear in mind the British Medical Association's Ethical Code which states: 'The doctor's basic duty is to preserve life, and there is no rigid code by which such considerations as quality of life can be taken into account when deciding appropriate treatment.'

It is not only doctors who seem to have claimed a right to kill the handicapped. There have been several cases of parents being acquitted of murder, while openly admitting that they did kill. One couple killed their brain damaged son, because, they said, he begged them to do it.[6] However, as they were the only ones who could understand his speech, we only have their word for that. Another woman killed her son who had cystic fibrosis. Despite the fact that the boy's father had applied for custody, so that the 'stress' of looking after him could have been immediately alleviated, the judge acquitted her, saying 'You were nothing other than caring and kind.'[7]

Some people of course, like Peter Singer and Helga Kuhse, think that this is quite acceptable. Their compatriot Michael Tooley went even further, saying that 'A newborn baby has no sense of self, so there is no moral difference between killing it and killing a kitten.'[8] Others believe that society's interests should come first, and that therefore, as handicapped children are burdensome, parents who refuse to 'listen to reason' should be overruled, and their children killed anyway.

A group called Prospect, who have close links to the Voluntary Euthanasia Society, tried a few years ago to legalise the killing of handicapped babies up to twenty-eight days old. One of their arguments was that such children prevent the birth of the potential future babies their parents might have had, if they were relieved of the burden of handicap.[9] This bizzare argument says in effect that people like me ought to be killed to protect the rights of those who don't even exist!

There are so many prejudicial things written these days about handicapped people, that it is hardly surprising that some parents begin to think their children would indeed be better off dead. We have already looked at some of them, in general terms; but the descriptions which new parents are often given of Down's children are even worse. They have 'simian lines on hands and feet, saddle noses, spade hands'. If the doctor is categorising their child in terms usually reserved for animals and inanimate objects, no wonder so many feel anxious or alarmed.

Professor Lorber describes people with my degree of spina bifida as 'dwarf, clumsy, often very fat, and have squints. They are socially isolated and will never have a chance to earn their own living, compete in open employment or be self supporting.'[10] This is quite untrue, but even if it were the case, do these qualities deserve the death penalty?

Many doctors seem to think they can foresee the future for handicapped babies. The only life we can judge and assess the value of is our own, and even that is only possible in retrospect. As long as the able bodied and those in power continue trying to make subjective statements about our potential we will never succeed in establishing ourselves as normal, equal human beings. Killing handicapped people can never be passed off as 'natural'. It is nothing short of a eugenic holocaust, despite fierce denials from its supporters. If babies may be killed because they are handicapped, and older handicapped or ill people can be killed because doctors think it's a reasonable thing for them to want, then we are very close indeed to the Nazi ideology.

It is sobering to remember that the Nazi holocaust began with killing the handicapped, whose lives were regarded as not only being worthless, but actually having a negative value. Children in concentration camps were often starved to death (which was also recorded then as 'natural death') and at the Nuremberg trials several doctors were imprisoned or even hanged for murdering them in this way. While I am firmly opposed to the death penalty, it is nevertheless interesting to observe that only forty years on, doctors are being praised for doing exactly the same thing.

Karl Binding and Alfred Hoche, whose book *The Destruction of Life Devoid of Value* set the tone for these killings, wrote: 'We doctors know that in the interests of the whole human organism single less valuable members have to be abandoned and pushed out. One more or less really does not matter much.'[11]

Under the Nazis, involuntary euthanasia quickly spread from the severely handicapped to those with 'odd shaped ears' or 'dark complexions'. Then it began to include also the politically or racially 'unfit'. Towards the end, Hermann Goering was heard to say, 'It's up to me to determine who is a Jew.' The whole holocaust started with the concept that there is such a thing as life unworthy of life. As Anne Frank wrote in her diary: 'If you define a person to be not a person, you do not have to feel pity.'

Supporters of voluntary euthanasia these days always lay great stress on the difference between voluntary and involuntary, and active and passive, euthanasia, but the distinctions are very blurred, particularly in the case of the newborn. Euthanasia is now openly practised in Holland, where doctors are not prosecuted for killing their patients. However, the whole facade of 'voluntary' euthanasia was belied by the statement of the Dutch Medical Association's Working Party that it is now considering the position of patients incapable of consenting. This would include handicapped newborns, the elderly insane and anyone else who might be considered unfit for life, but was unable to be eliminated 'voluntarily'.[12] It is almost as if death had been redefined as also meaning life with a handicap.

Judeo-Christian teaching is, thankfully, completely opposed to this. The Jewish view is that one minute of life is as valuable as one hundred years, and one life as precious as one million, since human life is of infinite value. Dr C. Everett Koop, Surgeon General of the United States, who is a committed Christian, extends this: 'We are constantly bombarded with the costs of keeping the handicapped and dying alive. I submit that the cost of all the handicapped, mentally and physically, is but a drop in the bucket compared to the cost of the morally handicapped.'[13]

Proverbs 21.13 (NEB) makes it quite clear who are the morally handicapped: 'If a man shuts his eyes to the cry of the helpless, he will cry for help himself and not be heard.' Perhaps we need to remember that, if we claim the right to kill someone because they are burdensome, we can't really say that they in turn should not be able to kill us, if we become a burden to them.

I'm not of course suggesting that futile treatments should be given to those who are obviously dying. But the aim must always be to assess the worth of the treatment to a particular person, and not the worth of the person to receive it. It is natural to want to die in the last stages of a terminal illness, but apart from that, requests for euthanasia usually come from people who are depressed, not those in physical pain.

Handicapped people actually commit suicide far less often than the able bodied; but those who try should surely be accorded the same treatment as anyone else who had a morbid desire to die. We don't say to someone able bodied who is about to take an overdose, 'Yes, you must be right. Let me help you.' However, if an absolute right to die was established, would we be forbidden to dissuade them? Would we allow chemists to sell a draught of hemlock to anyone who seemed to have been depressed for a long time? This is not a completely fanciful notion. Baroness Wootton claimed that a Bill introduced (fortunately unsuccessfully) by the Voluntary Euthanasia Society would have made it illegal to prevent some suicides.[14]

If some people with, say, spina bifida are happy and glad to be alive and others are not, it must be something other than the handicap which is causing the misery. There have been some tragic cases of handicapped people who have committed suicide, among them James Haig. He was paralysed in a motorcycle crash and, having been depressed for over a year, he set fire to his bungalow one day and died in the flames.[15] Advocates of euthanasia argue that this case, and others like it, prove that handicapped people should be allowed to be painlessly killed. But not everyone who is paralysed wants to die. What James Haig needed was to be treated for his depression, not killed because of his paralysis.

The same was true of Elizabeth Bouvia in the United States. She has cerebral palsy and decided her life was so awful she wanted to starve herself to death. She went to court to claim this right, which was denied. However, the psychiatrist who examined her found that she was actually suffering from clinical depression, and over subsequent months she repeatedly changed her mind about wanting to die.[16] People like Elizabeth need acceptance by society and the dignity of being treated as valuable, worthwhile people. There is not one human being alive who does not deserve to be treated in that way.

The fact that some people are handicapped, or do not have long left to live does not remove their human rights. Neither does it take away our responsibility to find ways of removing their fears and worries, without killing them. Time is only a relative concept and I am often reminded, when thinking about euthanasia, of the beautiful rose in Fontanelle's *Treatise on the Plurality of Worlds*, who stated that 'No gardener has ever been known to die.' There are possibilities we cannot even conceive of in life, but we will never discover them unless we accord each other the right to 'live until we die'.

In its 1988 Report on Euthanasia the BMA says:

> Contemporary culture worships bodily perfection and physical pleasure. This attitude to what makes a life worthwhile often dominates the thoughts of patients and their families when considering a new disability . . . However, the tradition in medicine is not to acquiesce to the shallow picture of human worth upon which these prejudices draw.[17]

Unfortunately, the report is rather inconsistent, as it then goes on to say that newborn handicapped children may be killed because of the 'harm many such infants do to the families into which they are born, and the often blighted and miserable lives which they lead.' Inconsistencies like this make a mockery of ethics. If older people and their families can learn to live with disability, so can those with congenital handicaps.

Christian people must surely agree that it is up to God to decide when death is appropriate, rather than allowing those who are too young, or depressed, or powerless to protest to be killed. Murder is killing in the best interests of someone other than the person who is going to die; and so, very often, is euthanasia. This is something everyone learns in earliest childhood – even if the big bad wolf *did* think Little Red Riding Hood and her Granny would be 'better off dead', no child reading the story would ever agree!

Some doctors claim that they are simply carrying out the dictum, 'Thou shalt not kill, but need'st not strive officiously to keep alive.' But maybe they ought to consider the poem in its proper context. It is called 'The Latest Decalogue' and was written by Arthur Clough, a minor nineteenth century poet and academic. It goes on to say: 'Thou shalt not steal, an empty feat, when it's so lucrative to cheat.' Hands up all those doctors who will admit to doing this!

The Voluntary Euthanasia Society, under its chairwoman Barbara Smoker has recently sent Living Wills to all its members, which they sign to say they do not want medical treatment if they contract certain conditions – another very worrying development. Ms Smoker makes the point that these wills can be revoked 'just as long as the patient is capable of some communication.' However, two very worrying possibilities remain. What if the patient is incapable of communicating, but *has* changed his mind? And what if he can't speak the same language as the doctor?

Fortunately there are some positive signs in amongst all this. The hospice movement has made good care of the terminally ill a practical reality, and it is very rare for patients in hospices to ask for euthanasia. If they do so, when questioned they almost invariably say, 'No, not now.

Only if the pain gets unbearable.' In hospices physical pain *can* be adequately controlled by prescribing appropriate pain killing drugs to be taken at regular intervals, before the pain ever recurs. This treatment is continued as long as it is beneficial to the patient.

Dame Cicely Saunders, founder of the hospice movement, maintains that euthanasia is 'unnecessary and an admission of defeat. You don't have to kill the patient to kill the pain.' Patients in hospices have a very good quality of life, are looked after in a caring, loving environment and visited by their families, children, even their pets. In Dame Cicely's words, 'Hospices are not about dying. They are about living until you die.'

There are also hospices for children who are dying. Matthew Nuckols, aged eleven and dying of multiple sclerosis, is a patient in one. He is confined to bed, his body terribly bloated due to his steroid treatment. He was very worried for his family, but the hospice has taught him that when his time comes he does not have to struggle: 'He won't be failing anyone if he just lets go.'[18]

Some dying children and adults can stay at home most of the time, helped either by their local hospice, the community nurses or by attendance at pain relief clinics which are now being established all over the country. How much happier and more dignified this is than the tragic situation of parents who kill their handicapped children because they are so worried about the future. With proper support, even the most severely handicapped of all – the comatose – can live and die peacefully and with real dignity. Karen Quinlan perhaps proved this best. She was removed from a respirator when it became obvious she would never recover from her coma, but she continued to live and breathe independently for ten years, until she died naturally.

New parents of handicapped children need care and support, not an offer to kill. The Contact-A-Family scheme set up to be a phone link for them to make contact with other families and support services or self help groups is the kind of thing that can make all the difference in this situation. The most important thing to remember, as always, is that no situation is completely without hope.

Janet Goodall, a consultant paediatrician in Stoke on Trent, and a friend who has helped me through many bad patches, said recently at the funeral of one of her handicapped patients, Claire:

There is disappointment, even dismay, when a child is found to be handicapped. Yet the oyster reminds us that pain can be transformed into something of great value; the little piece of grit, so irritating and distressing is slowly covered and changed into the pearl. The same thing can be true of handicap.

Perhaps some words from the Bible sum it up best:

I have set before you life and death, blessing and curses. Now choose life, so that you and your children may live.
(Deuteronomy 30.19 NIV)

Ask yourself

(1) Do you think euthanasia is ever justified? If so, under what conditions?

(2) Are Living Wills to be trusted?

(3) If voluntary euthanasia were allowed, should it also be available for people incapable of expressing their consent — i.e. old people, handicapped people with no speech, the newborn, those unable to communicate, those incapable of speaking the same language as the doctor?

(4) Is euthanasia an acceptable solution for severely depressed people?

(5) What are the alternatives to euthanasia?

(6) How can fit people best help the terminally ill and chronically sick? (Hint: Hospices always welcome more volunteer help.)

Conclusion

I hope that the conclusion to this book will already be apparent. Particularly if you have tried all the games and exercises in the various chapters, you will have at least an inkling of what disability feels like in certain situations. Hopefully, you will also have recognised the fact that many of the problems disabled people face are a direct result of a less than caring attitude on the part of an able bodied society.

'What can be done to change things?' is the question I hope most readers will want answered. There are several possibilities:

(1) The most important thing any able bodied person can do is to approach disabled people in a more sensitive way, regarding them not as frightening, or sad, or entirely different from 'normal' individuals, but rather, simply as people whose limitations are more outwardly apparent than those *you* suffer from.

We do have specific, practical needs, but these should be approached in a more egalitarian way than in the past. Do not help us because you feel sorry for us, or as a burdensome obligation. Do it as a demonstration of your belief that every human being is of infinite value and worth, and is equally entitled to participate in society.

(2) Remember that we generally want to lead ordinary lives, and join in with different activities, not always to be pushed aside into 'special' facilities and organisations. Don't leave us out!

(3) Consider when you go out shopping, or to school, college or work, 'Could a disabled person do this?' If not, why? Could anything be done to improve matters? If new buildings in your area – shops, libraries, churches, schools, pubs – are not accessible to disabled people, write to the local council and find out why, registering your concern.

Demonstrate your unwillingness to accept an environment which excludes disabled people, by getting involved with the struggle for equal access. In a civilised, Christian community this should be something everyone is involved in, not just those who actually have a disability.

(4) Learn finger-spelling! It is quick and easy to do, and you could help a deaf person enormously by knowing the rudiments of their language. Teach your family and friends too.

(5) Be more sensitive to the problems facing people who acquire disabilities later in life. It is hard enough for them to come to terms with their own altered abilities, without also having to cope with negative attitudes from those they come into contact with.

(6) Be aware of the poverty which affects so many disabled people. There are five million disabled people in Britain, and 65 per cent of them live below the poverty line. They are two-and-a-half times more likely to be unemployed than the able bodied, and the education many receive in special schools is inappropriate for a competitive, fast-moving world. Government disability allowances are inadequate, and recent changes to the Social Security Act mean that many disabled people will simply not have the financial resources to leave their parents' homes or institutions and live independently in the community. What can you do to help balance this terrible inequality in wealth? Write to your MP and tell him that disabled people want, and deserve, as of right, an adequate, secure income.

(7) Remember the needs of those with 'marginal' disabilities. Don't make jokes about epilepsy, or incontinence, or mental handicap, and register your objections when others do. It isn't funny to the people affected. What is needed in order to make such people feel secure, accepted and wanted is tolerance and understanding – actually things every human being needs.

(8) Bear in mind that the handicapped are now threatened by abortion and neo-natal euthanasia. Let us not forget the lessons the Nazi experience taught. How can disabled people ever be accepted and valued in a society which so openly prefers to kill disabled babies at the earliest possible

moment? Join the pro-life movement, and help secure the future for unborn children, both handicapped and able bodied.

(9) Don't forget that handicapped people can teach you things too – if you are willing to listen. My handicap is not the most important thing about me, and there are other interests I have which are just as much a part of who I am as the fact that I have spina bifida.

Some people with little experience of handicap find this hard to understand, and seem to think the only thing disabled people really know about is disability. Wrong! While writing this book I have also: Read twenty-six books, learned a new Chopin étude on the piano, visited friends, and had a lot of different people to stay at my house, continued my Spanish lessons (in preparation for a projected trip to South America next year), and started to teach myself Sinhalese. This latter is in order to write to my foster child, Sriyanee, who lives in Sri Lanka, in her own language. This is all, of course, in addition to my full time work writing and speaking on the right to life of people with disabilities. So talk to me about things other than handicap – I want to learn new ideas and different aspects of what the world has to offer.

(10) Cultivate a non-fearful, non-discriminatory attitude to disability. It is society's reactions, not physical or mental disability in itself, which severely handicap us.

Finally, note the words of the philosopher Schopenhauer: 'It is in the overcoming of obstacles that one feels the full delight of existence.'

Notes

INTRODUCTION
1 J. Hastings (Ed.), *Encyclopaedia of Religion and Ethics*, Edinburgh, T. & T. Clark, vol. 5, p. 443
2 Alastair Campbell and Roger Higgs, *In That Case*

1 PEOPLE WITH DISABILITIES
1 J. Campling (Ed.) *Images of Ourselves: Women with Disabilities Talking*, London, Routledge and Kegan Paul, 1981
2 Quoted in *Link* (magazine of the Association for Spina Bifida and Hydrocephalus), nos. 57–59, 1978
3 Personal correspondence. Also *Parents* magazine, February 1988
4 *Link*, loc. cit.
5 *General Practitioner*, February 1982
6 Linda Scotson, *Doran*, Pan, 1985
7 Quoted in *Combat* (magazine of the Huntington's Chorea Society), Spring 1988
8 Reported in *The Times*, 25th and 26th February 1984
9 Personal contact
10 *Woman* magazine, June 1988
11 *In From the Cold* (magazine of the Liberation Network of People with Disabilities), Spring 1985
12 Reported in *The Times*, 26th January 1988
13 Reported in the *Daily Mail*, 16th June 1987
14 Christian Care for the Mentally Handicapped (Acorn Trust) leaflet.
15 SPUC Handicap Division Newsletter, Winter 1987/8

2 THE RIGHT TO LEARN
1 Tom Booth and Will Swann (Eds.), *Including Pupils with Disabilities*, Oxford University Press, 1987

2 *Growing up with Spina Bifida*, Scottish Spina Bifida Association booklet
3 Reported in local newspaper, Weston-super-Mare, 12th July 1988
4 SPUC Handicap Division Newsletter, Spring 1985

3 CASTLES IN THE AIR
1 *Link*, 5th June 1983
2 Debby Hill, *Timothy: Mission Accomplished* (unpublished manuscript)
3 *Link Focus on Housing*

4 JOBS FOR THE BOYS?
1 International Federation for Hydrocephalus and Spina Bifida, *Focus*, Spring 1988
2 Personal correspondence
3 SPUC Handicap Division Newsletter, Winter 1987/8

5 GETTING THERE
1 Reported in the *Sun*, 17th April 1985
2 CORAD (Committee on Restrictions against Disabled People) Report November 1983
3 Reported in the *Star*, 29th November 1984
4 CORAD report as above
5 Reported in the *Sydney Morning Herald*, 19th April 1988
6 Martin Luther King, *Chaos or Community?*, London, Hodder and Stoughton, 1967

6 SEE WHAT I MEAN?
1 SENSE leaflet
2 Quoted in *Everywoman*, August 1985
3 Reported in *News of the World*, 20th March 1988
4 Ann Lovell, *Simple Simon*, Lion, 1983
5 Reported in the *Guardian*, 10th October 1984
6 Marie Rothenburg and Mel White, *David*, Kingsway 1985
7 Quoted in Mary Craig, *Blessings*, Hodder and Stoughton, 1979

8 Disabled Women for Life leaflet, *Attitudes to People with Mental Handicap*

7 YOUR WORST FEARS REALISED
1 Two-headed babies were variously reported in Teheran, Iran (*Sunday Sport*, 6th January 1988); in Italy (*Sunday Sport*, 3rd April 1988); in Mogadishu, Somalia (*Sun*, 20th April 1988
2 Reported in the *Guardian*, 8th September 1981
3 Article by Polly Toynbee, the *Guardian*, 10th March 1988
4 Polly Toynbee in the *Guardian*, 7th July 1988
5 See my paper on *The Status of Anacephalic Babies*: Should their Bodies be Used as Donor Banks?, *Journal of Medical Ethics*, September 1988. (This is the text of a debate in which I took part at St Mary's Hospital, London in November 1987)
6 Quoted in *Today*, 14th July 1987
7 Francis Schaeffer and C. Everett Koop, *Whatever Happened to the Human Race?* Marshall, Morgan and Scott, 1983
8 J. Campling, *Better Lives for Disabled Women*, Virago, 1979
9 Quoted in the *People*, 24th November 1985

8 THE SLIPPERY SLOPE
1 *British Medical Journal* 1981, anonymous letter
2 *The Times*, 9th May 1988
3 Quoted in *Woman* magazine, August 1988
4 Parliamentary debate on the Second Hearing of David Alton's Abortion Amendment Bill, *Hansard*, 22nd January 1988
5 The case of 'Jeanette.' SPUC Handicap Division Newsletter, Winter 1987/8
6 *The Times*, 24th September 1987
7 Royal College of Obstetrics and Gynaecology Ethics Committee Report 1985
8 *British Medical Journal*, 9th July 1988
9 William Liley, *The Tiniest Humans*, Robert Sassone, 1977

10 Institute of Medical Ethics Bulletin, February 1988
11 Standing Committee D on Unborn Children (Protection) Bill, Third sitting 13th March 1985. House of Commons Official Report, HMSO
12 Martin Luther King, *Chaos or Community?*

10 OVER MY DEAD BODY!

 1 Judge's summing up of the Doctor Arthur trial, November 1981
 2 Reported in the *Guardian*, 25th February 1981
 3 Reported in the *Guardian*, 21st June 1988
 4 Personal correspondence. Also *Journal of Medical Ethics*, July 1988
 5 Ibid.
 6 Reported in the *Sun*, 15th May 1985
 7 Reported in the *Daily Express*, 5th August 1985
 8 M. Tooley, *Abortion*
 9 Madeleine Simms, 'Severely Handicapped Infants: A Discussion Document', written for Prospect 1981
10 *Link* magazine. (*Link* Special Supplement, *Lives in Question*, 1981. Also personal correspondence.
11 Karl Binding and Alfred Hoche, *The Release of the Destruction of Lives Devoid of Value*, Leipzig 1920. Also Robert Sassone's commentary on the above, 1975
12 British Medical Association News Review January 1986, *An Open and Gentle Death* by Dr John Dawson, Head of the BMA's Professional and Scientific Division
13 Schaeffer and Koop, *Whatever Happened to the Human Race?*
14 House of Lords Debate on the Suicide Amendment Bill, 11th December 1985. Baroness Wootton is a member of the Voluntary Euthanasia Society.
15 The *Guardian*, 25th April 1983. Article by Polly Toynbee
16 The *Daily Telegraph*, 7th January 1984
17 Dame Cicely Saunders, British Medical Association Euthanasia Report, 21st April 1988
18 Reported in *You*, July 1988

Bibliography

Booth, Tom and Swan, Will (Eds.), *Including Pupils with Disabilities*, Oxford University Press, 1987

British Medical Association, *Handbook of Medical Ethics*, BMA, 1984

Carr, Marilyn, *Look No Hands*, Canongate Publishing, 1982

Craig, Mary, *Blessings*, Hodder and Stoughton, 1979

Henderson, Peter, *Disability in Childhood and Youth*, Oxford University Press, 1974

Hunt, Nigel, *The World of Nigel Hunt*, Asset Recycling, 1982

Kennedy, Ian, *The Unmasking of Medicine*, Paladin, 1981

Linacre Centre, *Euthanasia and Clinical Practice*, 1982

Lovell, Ann, *Simple Simon*, Lion, 1983

Masham, Susan, *The World Walks By*, Collins, 1986

Sanctuary, Gerald, *After I'm Gone*, Souvenir Press, 1984

Scotson, Linda, *Doran*, Pan, 1985

Shakespeare, Rosemary, *The Psychology of Handicap*, Methuen, 1975

Williams, Christopher and Susan, *Cancer – A Guide for Patients and their Families*, John Wiley and Sons

Useful Addresses

(* Denotes pro-life group)

AFASIC (Speech Impairments), 347 Central Market, Smithfield, London EC1A 9NH. Tel: 01–236 3632/6487

Association for Independent Disabled Self Sufficiency, 7 Alfred Street, Bath, Avon BA1 2QU. Tel: 0225 25197

Association for Spina Bifida and Hydrocephalus, 22 Upper Woburn Place, London WC1H 0EP. Tel: 01–388 1382

Association of Parents of Vaccine-Damaged Children, 2 Church Street, Shipston on Stour, Warwicks CV36 4AP. Tel: 0608 61595

Association to Combat Huntington's Chorea (COMBAT), Borough House, 34A Station Road, Hinckley, Leics LE10 1AP. Tel: 0455 615558

Barnardo's, Tanners Lane, Barkingside, Ilford, Essex IG6 1QG. Tel: 01–550 8822

British Agencies for Adoption and Fostering (BAAF), 11 Southwark Street, London SE1 1RQ. Tel: 01–407 8800

British Association of Cancer United Patients and their Families and Friends (BACUP), 121/123 Charterhouse Street, London EC1M 6AA. Tel: 01–608 1785 (Cancer Information Service 9.30–5 Mon, Wed, Fri., 9.30–7 Tu, Th.)

British Diabetic Association, 10 Queen Anne Street, London W1M 0BD. Tel: 01–323 1531

British Epilepsy Association, Anstey House, Hanover Square, Leeds LS3 1BE. Tel: 0532 439393

British Polio Fellowship, Bell Close, West End Road, Ruislip HA4 6LP. Tel: 0895 675515

Brittle Bone Society, Unit 4, Block 20, Carlunie Road, Dundee DD2 3QT. Tel: 0382 817771

Campaign for Mentally Handicapped People, 12a Maddox Street, London W1R 9PL. Tel: 01–491 0727

* CARE (Christian Action, Research and Education), 53 Romney Street, London SW1P 3RF. Tel: 01–233 0455

Carers National Association, 29 Chilworth Mews, London W2 3RG. Tel: 01–724 7776

Catholic Handicapped Childrens Fellowship, 2 The Villas, Hare Law, Stanley, Co. Durham DH9 8DQ. Tel: 0207 234379

*Christian Concern for the Mentally Handicapped (Acorn Trust), PO Box 351, Reading RG1 7AL. Tel: 0734 508781

Conductive Education, University of Birmingham, PO Box 363, Birmingham B15 2TT. Tel: 021 414 4947/8

Contact-A-Family (Linking families with a handicapped child), 16 Strutton Ground, London SW1P 2HP. Tel: 01–222 2695

Crossroads (Care Attendant Schemes), 10 Regent Place, Rugby, Warwicks CV21 2PN. Tel: 0788 73653

Cystic Fibrosis Research Trust, Alexandra House, 5 Blyth Road, Bromley, Kent BR1 3RS. Tel: 01–464 7211/2

DIAL UK (Disablement Information Advice Line), 117 High Street, Clay Cross, Chesterfield, Derbyshire S45 9DZ. Tel: 0246 250055

Disability Alliance (Information on Rights and Benefits), 25 Denmark Street, London WC2H 8NJ. Tel: 01–240 0806

Disabled Christians Fellowship, 50 Clare Road, Kingswood, Bristol BS15 1PJ. Tel: 0272 616141

Disabled Drivers' Association, Ashwellthorpe Hall, Ashwellthorpe, Norwich NR16 1EX. Tel: 050 841 449

Disabled Living Foundation, 380–384 Harrow Road, London W9 2HU. Tel: 01 289 6111

Disablement Income Group, Millmead Business Centre, Millmead Road, London N17 9QU. Tel: 01–801 8013

Down's Syndrome Association, 12–13 Clapham Common, Southside, London SW4 7AA. Tel: 01 720 0008

Dystrophic Epidermolysis Bullosa Research Association, Suit 4, 1 Kings Road, Crowthorne, Berks RG11 7BG. Tel: 0344 771961

Equipment for the Disabled, Mary Marlborough Lodge, Nuffield Orthopaedic Centre, Headington, Oxford OX3 7LD. Tel: 0865 750103

Family Fund (Financial assistance for families on low incomes with severely handicapped children), Joseph Rowntree Memorial Trust, PO Box 50, York YO1 1UY. Tel: 0904 621115

Friedreich's Ataxia Group, The Common, Cranleigh, Surrey GU6 8SB. Tel: 0483 272741

Haemophilia Society, 123 Westminster Bridge Road, London SE1 7HR. Tel: 01–928 2020

*Handicapped Children's Pilgrimage Trust, 100A High Street, Banstead, Surrey SM7 2RB. Tel: 0737 353311

Ileostomy Association of Great Britain and Ireland, Central Office, Amblehurst House, Black Scotch Lane, Mansfield Notts NG18 4PF.

In Touch (Comprehensive information service on mental handicap and rare disorders), 10 Norman Road, Sale, Cheshire M33 3DF. Tel: 061 962 4441

John Grooms Association for the Disabled, 10 Gloucester Drive, Finsbury Park, London N4 2LP. Tel: 01–802 7272

Leonard Cheshire Foundation, 26–29 Maunsel Street, London SW1P 2QN. Tel: 01–828 1822

Leukaemia Care Society, PO Box 82, Exeter EX2 5DP. Tel: 0392 218514

*LIFE, 118–120 Warwick Street, Leamington Spa, Warwicks CV32 4QY. Tel: 0926 21587

MENCAP, 123 Golden Lane, London EC1Y 0RT. Tel: 01–253 9433

MIND, 22 Harley Street, London W1N 2ED. Tel: 01–637 0741

Multiple Sclerosis Society, 25 Effie Road, London SW6 1EE. Tel: 01–736 6267

Muscular Dystrophy Group, Nattrass House, 35 Macaulay Road, London SW4 0QP. Tel: 01–720 8055

National Ankylosing Spondylitis Society, 6, Grosvenor Crescent, London SW1X 7ER. Tel: 01–235 9585

National Autistic Society, 276 Willesden Lane, London NW2 5RB. Tel: 01–451 1114

National Deaf/Blind Helpers League, 18 Rainbow Court, Paston Ridings, Peterborough PE4 6UP. Tel: 0773 73511

Northern Ireland Council on Disability, 2 Annadale Avenue, Belfast BT7 3TR. Tel: 0232 640011

OPUS (Organisation for Parents under Stress), 106 Godstone Road, Whyteleafe, Surrey CR3 0EB. Tel: 01–645 0469

Parkinson's Disease Society, 36 Portland Place, London W1N 3DG. Tel: 01–255 2432

PHAB (Physically Handicapped and Able Bodied Clubs), Tavistock House North (2nd Floor), Tavistock Square, London WC1H 9WX. Tel: 01–388 1963

Portage and Home Teaching Association (for handicapped children), Department of Psychology, University of Southampton

Possum Users Association, 160 De la Warr Road, Bexhill-on-Sea, East Sussex. Tel: 0424 217093

RADAR (Royal Association for Disability and Rehabilitation), 25 Mortimer Street, London W1N 8AB. Tel: 01–637 5400

Red Cross, 9 Grosvenor Crescent, London SW1X 7EJ. Tel: 01–235 5454

Royal National Institute for the Blind, 224 Great Portland Street, London W1N 6AA. Tel: 01–388 1266

Royal National Institute for the Deaf, 105 Gower Street, London WC1E 6AH. Tel: 01–387 8033

Schizophrenia Fellowship, 78–9 Victoria Road, Surbiton, Surrey KT6 4NS. Tel: 01–390 3651/2

Scottish Council on Disability, Princes House, 5 Shandwick Place, Edinburgh EH2 4RG. Tel: 031 229 8632

SENSE (Society for deaf/blind and rubella handicapped people), 311 Grays Inn Road, London WC1X 8PT. Tel: 01–278 1005

Skill: National Bureau for Students with Disabilities, 336 Brixton Road, London SW9 7AA. Tel: 01–274 0565

Spastics Society, 12 Park Crescent, London W1N 4EQ. Tel: 01–636 5020

Special Care Agency (Care Assistants for parents with handicapped children), 1st Floor, 45 Pembridge Road, London W11 3HG. Tel: 01–221 5894

Spinal Injuries Association, Newpoint, 76 St James's Lane, London N10 3DF. Tel: 01–444 2121

SPOD (Sexual Problems of the Disabled), 286 Camden Road, London N7 0BJ. Tel: 01–607 8851/2

*Society for the Protection of Unborn Children (Handicap Division), 7 Tufton Street, Westminster, London SW1P 3QN. Tel: 01–222 5845

Urostomy Association, Buckland, Beaumont Park, Danbury, Essex CM3 4DE.

Voluntary Council for Handicapped children (Advice service on all aspects of childhood disability and sources of help), 8 Wakley Street, London EC1V 7QE. Tel: 01–278 9441

Wales Council for the Disabled, Caerbragdy Industrial Estate, Bedwas Road, Caerphilly, Mid-Glamorgan CF8 3SL. Tel: 0222 887325

The Standard Manual Alphabet

(Reproduced by courtesy of the Royal National Institute for the Deaf)